Execution

LARRY BOSSIDY is chairman and CEO of Honeywell International, Inc. Honeywell is a $25 billion diversified technology and manufacturing leader. Bossidy had served as chairman and CEO of AlliedSignal from 1991 to 1999, when he became chairman of Honeywell following the merger of AlliedSignal and Honeywell in December 1999. He retired from the company in April 2000 and returned as chairman and CEO in July 2001.

Bossidy is credited with transforming AlliedSignal into one of the world's most admired companies, whose success was largely driven by an intense focus on growth and Six Sigma–driven productivity. During his tenure with Allied-Signal the company achieved consistent growth in earnings and cash flow, highlighted by 31 consecutive quarters of earnings-per-share growth of 13 percent or more.

Before joining AlliedSignal, Bossidy served in a number of executive and financial positions with General Electric Company, which he joined as a trainee in 1957. He was Chief Operating Officer of General Electric Credit Corporation (now GE Capital Corporation) from 1979 to 1981, Executive Vice President and President of GE's Services and Materials Sector from 1981 to 1984, and Vice Chairman and Executive Officer of General Electric Company from 1984 to July 1991.

RAM CHARAN is a highly sought adviser to CEOs and senior executives in companies ranging from start-ups to the *Fortune* 500, including GE, Ford, DuPont, EDS, Universal Studios, and Verizon. He is the author of *What the CEO Wants You to Know* and *Boards at Work* and the coauthor of *Every Business Is a Growth Business* and *The Leadership Pipeline*. Dr. Charan has written numerous articles for *Harvard Business Review* and *Fortune* magazine, has a D.B.A. and M.B.A. from Harvard Business School, and has taught at both Harvard and Northwestern.

CHARLES BURCK is a writer and editor who has worked with Ram Charan on several books, including *Every Business Is a Growth Business*. Earlier in his career he was an editor at *Fortune* magazine.

EXECUTION

THE DISCIPLINE OF GETTING THINGS DONE

**LARRY BOSSIDY AND
RAM CHARAN**

with Charles Burck

BUSINESS
BOOKS

Published by Random House Business Books 2011

13

First published in Great Britain in 2002 by Random House Business Books

This revised edition first published in the United States in 2009 by Crown
Business, an imprint of the Crown Publishing Group, a division of Random
House, Inc., New York, and in Great Britain in 2011 by
Random House Business Books

Random House, 20 Vauxhall Bridge Road,
London SW1V 2SA

www.rbooks.co.uk

Addresses for companies within The Random House Group Limited can be
found at: www.randomhouse.co.uk/offices.htm

The Random House Group Limited Reg. No. 954009

A CIP catalogue record for this book
is available from the British Library

ISBN 9781847940681

Printed and bound in India by
Replika Press Pvt. Ltd.

To the hundreds of people who touched our business lives and influenced the thoughts articulated in this book. A special recognition to Jack Welch, who in our time was the predominant practitioner of "getting things done."

Larry Bossidy
Ram Charan

What's your
masterpiece?

Go Beout.

Cm

CONTENTS

Resetting *Execution* for a Time of Crisis   ix

Introduction   1

PART I: WHY EXECUTION IS NEEDED

1: The Gap Nobody Knows   13

2: The Execution Difference   35

PART II: THE BUILDING BLOCKS OF EXECUTION

3: Building Block One: The Leader's Seven
Essential Behaviors   57

4: Building Block Two: Creating the
Framework for Cultural Change   85

5: Building Block Three: The Job No Leader
Should Delegate—Having the Right People
in the Right Place   109

PART III: THE THREE CORE PROCESSES OF EXECUTION

6: The People Process: Making the Link with Strategy and Operations   141

7: The Strategy Process: Making the Link with People and Operations   178

8: How to Conduct a Strategy Review   207

9: The Operations Process: Making the Link with Strategy and People   226

Conclusion: Letter to a New Leader   265

Index   271

RESETTING EXECUTION FOR A TIME OF CRISIS

Execution, when first published in 2002, was based on our observation that the discipline of getting things done was what differentiated companies that succeeded from those that just muddled through or failed.

Today we are mired in a deep global recession that is taking a tremendous toll on businesses, consumers, and governments. Everywhere there is a huge loss of confidence. Strategies and business models that once worked well no longer do so. Even when the recession ends the business and economic environment will not return to what we have come to regard as "normal."

The world is experiencing a tectonic shift—the global business environment is being "reset." We now live in a world in which radical change can happen seemingly overnight, and in which many former "givens" will be in flux for a long time. That reality makes execution harder (not that it's ever been easy), but also more important than ever before. Execution not only ensures efficient use of resources in a credit and cash-starved world, but also provides the feedback loop needed for the business to adjust to changes—big or small—in the external world. True, leaders must still conceive of a path forward, but execution is what drives the organization along that path and allows it to seize opportunities. And good execution not only will see a company through the tough times, but also significantly improve its chances for success as the environment continues to shift.

No one can predict precisely what the future holds—we will all have to deal with whatever is ahead when it happens—but consider some of the more profound changes that are likely to be in store:

- *Growth will be slower.* The vast consumer market that is America may no longer be the principal global economic driver it has been, and countries intent on creating jobs for their people will be much slower to import our goods. During the early stages of recovery from the recession, credit will still be constrained, leverage restricted, and opportunities for profitable growth difficult to find. But the company that executes well will have the confidence, speed, and resources to move fast as new opportunities emerge. It will also have credibility as a partner, supplier, and investment of choice, compounding its advantage as it positions itself for growth.

- *Competition will be fiercer.* In a slower-growth global economy everyone will be fighting harder and smarter to win market share. Each company will be searching for a new advantage, in the form of products, technologies, management, locations, prices, among many other variables. The margins for error are thinner, and flexibility and speed in assigning and re-assigning resources will make a huge difference in performance. That's a lot to contend with and faulty execution in these basic performance nuts and bolts can lead to a death sentence, but that's not all. Stronger, faster companies can detect and pounce on opportunities, for instance, to take advantage of the downturn by snapping up assets at bargain prices and snatching market share out from under their competitors. Good execution reveals flaws in outmoded or wrong strategies sooner and allows time to change direction. Those who fail to see the errors in their strategies or who fail to execute the correct strategies quickly and effectively will face the fate that confronted GM, Chrysler, Bear Stearns, AIG, and Lehman Brothers as the economic and financial crises unfolded.

- *Governments around the world will take new roles in their economies and business environments.* There will be a new regulatory environment and each government will carry it out in different ways, some as partners to business, others as adversaries. But there is also a trend toward more global rather than national regulation and that could present formidable obstacles given the various cultures and political systems involved in such a widespread effort. Even regulation at the national level will be heavily influenced by who the regulators are and what credibility they have. And there will invariably be calls for protectionism to shelter jobs and markets that suffer from intensifying competitive pressures. Companies that execute well will be more attractive as partners and suppliers to government bodies and better prepared to adapt to changing regulations.

- *Risk management—understanding and controlling risks at every level of the business, including political and global economic risk—will become a huge part of every leader's job.* As of this writing there is considerable debate about whether the global economy will slide into deflation or if stimulus policies will touch off a new burst of inflation. Being prepared for either result is a fundamental tenet of risk management. But inflation or deflation can be forecast to some extent. The real risks are those that lie hidden beneath the veneer of "business as usual." A decade ago credit default obligations or collateralized mortgage obligations mattered little, yet those instruments, highly touted a few years ago as a means to reduce risk, have been at the root of the current crisis. The lesson of the past two years is clear: Your strategy must incorporate a plan to deal with not only company and industry-specific risks, but also unknown risks, such as those in the global financial system. Execution is what gives you an edge in detecting new realities in the external environment as well as risks that are being introduced, perhaps inadvertantly, to your own operations.

■ ■ ■

Execution done well makes a huge difference in a company's performance, as we have seen with the way in which Richard T. Clark has changed Merck & Co. since becoming chairman and CEO of the giant pharmaceutical firm in 2005. The board chose Clark because it was looking for someone well grounded in both medicine and operations. Clark had demonstrated an ability to execute first as head of Merck's manufacturing operations, then as the leader of its Medco Health Solutions subsidiary.

When Clark took over the top role, Merck was floundering. Its strategy was little more than an expanded vision statement containing broad general statements about how good Merck was. It was little more than platitudes, a strategy in name only. Without a real strategy against which to execute, Merck was not moving forward. Almost immediately Clark undertook an extensive review of Merck's business, selecting the areas in which it would have the best chance of winning given its research abilities and history. Once he targeted the right areas, Clark put the company through a rigorous analysis of its existing manufacturing facilities and technology to choose the plants and technologies that would become the foundation for his strategy of innovation and excellence. He provided meaning to these otherwise vague terms by ensuring that Merck's manufacturing arm could anticipate technological developments and seize a position at the cutting edge of innovation in the fields that Merck would pursue. The company's history and performance argued strongly, for example, to maintain a commanding position in cardiology.

With a real strategy in place Clark then made extensive changes in the top ranks of management to ensure that Merck's leadership both knew what the strategy was and could execute it as a team. And when his internal organization was up and running the way he wanted it to, Clark took yet another major step and engineered the acquisition of Schering-Plough, a major coup. In short, Clark used each of the three core processes of execution and made sure that they were linked together so that the company's priorities and allocation of resources were aligned with its reorganization and sharper focus. Clark, a low-key leader, altered Merck's entire culture quickly and efficiently, demonstrating that leaders need not be loud and bombastic to command respect and achieve results.

THE THREE CORE PROCESSES OF EXECUTION

The three processes—people, strategy, and operations—remain the building blocks and heart of good execution. But as the economic, political, and business environments change, the ways in which they are carried out also change.

Strategy

The ground rules for formulating strategy are shifting rapidly as the world resets. The global crisis that began in earnest in 2008 demonstrates conclusively that it will no longer be sufficient to develop a strategy based only on competitive industry analysis. Rather, every strategy needs to take into account the ever-changing environment for global business.

One need look no further than Russia to see how quickly business conditions can change. Just two years ago Russia appeared to be one of the most promising places on earth for business development. Now it is an economic and political wreck and much apprehension exists about its business future. And while China was the place to go for manufacturing ten years ago, today it is far from the most competitive supplier of goods while Mexico, which many years ago was the original location for outsourcing, looms large again today as a potential sourcing location given its proximity to the United States.

Decisions about strategy are not, of course, limited to mega-issues such as which countries to do business in, but include those of day-to-day importance such as constantly questioning the selection of vendors and whether they still fit into a company's evolving supply chain strategy.

It is imperative, too, that every strategy takes into account an analysis and understanding of the global financial and economic environment marked by slower growth, increased competition, altered consumer behavior, and more government intervention. All of those are tantamount to increased risk at every level, and those risks must be better understood and taken into account in the formulation of a strategy.

People

An environment of fast growth can cover a multitude of sins, but an era of slow growth will magnify every shortcoming of every person in the business, especially the leaders. Not only will many formerly well-regarded managers be found wanting in the new environment, there will also be a shortage of well-grounded leaders who have the mental acuity, fortitude, and persistence to execute well in a tough environment.

Leaders must be sensitive to when a strategy has run its course and needs to be changed and have the flexibility to act quickly to make the change. The consequences of not doing so can be fatal. For example, Richard Fuld, the chairman of Lehman Brothers, stubbornly held onto his strategy of high leverage for months after the Bear Stearns bankruptcy revealed its flaws. Fuld simply failed to see how the collapsing mortgage market would affect the company in time to do anything about it. Failure was the result, a failure that jeopardized the global financial order.

Competition for the best leaders will be intense. One way to ensure that you have the right people in the right jobs in this rapidly shifting environment is by writing job descriptions for the kind of people you need in each job as it will exist *tomorrow,* then match those descriptions against the talents and abilities of the peole holding those jobs *today.* If you don't have the right leaders for the environment, then it is incumbent to move quickly and make the necessary changes. You must also begin now to cultivate the leaders of the future, testing and evaluating people for their ability to execute in the face of new challenges and circumstances.

Operations

To execute well there must be accountability, clear goals, accurate methods to measure performance, and the right rewards for people who perform. But now, more than ever before, leaders need to design flexible operating plans. In the past a company might make one or perhaps two profound changes in its operations each year. But in the future such changes, whether rebalancing inventories, readjusting prices, or reformulating advertising and marketing plans, may occur several times in a year and the operating plan must be able to adopt by rapidly moving resources from one place to another. In the late 1990s PepsiCo spun off its bottling operations based largely on a financial engineering plan whose logic ultimately failed. Then in 2009 PepsiCo chairwoman Indra Nooyi reversed course and offered to buy back the bottling operations to provide the necessary operating flexibility and regain control of operating and distribution costs.

Strategy no longer is set in stone. A good strategy will be under constant review or revision depending on what is happening in the business environment. And as the strategy changes, so, too, must the company's people and operations. Leaders should not seek change for change's sake, but they and everyone else in the company need to be prepared to change quickly when conditions dictate a change. Change might come in the form of a geographic shift in sourcing, away from China and toward Mexico, for instance. And people need to understand that major changes will affect them in unexpected ways. When Procter & Gamble decided to shift from a global to a regional structure around the world, the change required a different set of people in leadership positions. It wasn't that the people already in place weren't doing a good job, but the new mandate required different skills and knowledge.

EXECUTION IN THE REAL WORLD

It's not enough to simply get one, two, or even all three of the processes right. Linkage between all three is crucial as we illustrate by examining the results obtained by the leaders of two of our largest financial institutions: Jamie Dimon, chairman of JPMorgan Chase, and Charles Prince, the former CEO of CitiGroup. Both are respected, smart, and capable. But their execution took their organizations to two very different places.

Consider first their backgrounds. Jamie was the son of Theodore "Ted" Dimon, a star stock broker at Shearson and a close friend of Sandy Weill, the imaginative and hard driving financier who would eventually put together the deal that created CitiGroup. Weill took the young Dimon under his wing, first as a gofer during summer breaks from college, then as sort of an executive assistant. As Weill's career soared, Dimon continued as his understudy, watching not only how Weill evaluated companies in minute detail, but also how he worked with and evaluated people. Even when Weill was ousted from American Express and went into a form of executive exile, Dimon stayed with him, strategizing ways the duo could get back into the financial business and running the numbers on potential deals. Together they launched an ambitious effort to turn a failing finance company, Commercial Credit, into a vehicle that would enable them to reach the pinnacle of the financial world. Through a series of mergers and acquisitions engineered by Weill and Dimon, Commercial Credit eventually became CitiGroup. Up until the day in 1998 that Weill ousted his young protégé from CitiGroup, Dimon was learning about every aspect of the finance business, from the smallest details to the grandest of strategies. Not surprisingly, he could pick and choose among jobs offered him, and in 2000 he became chief executive officer of BankOne, then the nation's fifth largest bank. JPMorgan's acquisition of BankOne in 2004 paved the way for Dimon to become chairman of JPMorgan Chase.

Charles Prince also worked closely with Sandy Weill, although he came to that position much differently than Dimon did. Prince, the son of a plasterer and a housewife, started his career as an attorney with U.S. Steel Corp. as that company was floundering under the impact of foreign competition. He then joined Commercial Credit in 1979 as it, too, stumbled. One of his jobs as the company's lawyer was to find someone to buy Commercial Credit from its owner, Control Data. He found that virtually impossible until 1986 when Sandy Weill and Jamie Dimon pinpointed Commercial Credit as their chosen vehicle to reclaim their status on Wall Street. Despite tough negotiations over the purchase, Weill came away respectful of Prince's good humor and attention to detail. Prince then became the mediator between the demoralized employees of Commercial Credit and the aggressive team that Weill put together to make the company profitable. And while Prince also played an important role in the evaluation of potential mergers and acquisitions proposed by Weill and Dimon, he was not deeply involved in the day-to-day business operations of Commercial Credit or of the subsequent companies that eventually became CitiGroup. Once Jamie Dimon had been ousted from CitiGroup, Prince became Weill's chief confidante and protector as Enron and WorldCom, two CitiGroup clients, collapsed amidst massive fraud. Weill handpicked Prince to succeed him, and the lawyer became CEO in 2003 and chairman of CitiGroup in 2006.

Dimon and Prince took two very different approaches to their jobs as the heads of major financial institutions. At JPMorgan Dimon took a methodical approach to execution:

- He established very clear *profit-and-loss responsibilities* for each division of the bank down to the *lowest levels feasible*. Each division was ordered to *benchmark itself against the best of its competitors* in the same business. (None of JPMorgan's businesses were regarded at the time as the best in its business).

- He carefully evaluated the people from both BankOne and JPMorgan to *select the best* to run each business, choosing BankOne's consumer banking executive to run JPMorgan's consumer unit and JPMorgan's head of investment banking to run the combined investment banking business. He also reached back into

CitiGroup to recruit some of its best consumer banking experts, people with whom he had worked closely before his ouster.

- He *invested heavily in information technology* to keep track of the burgeoning consumer and investment banking businesses and their need for fast, accurate, and thorough information that could give them a competitive edge.

- He set up *rigorous compensation policies* that made it clear that if the company overall didn't thrive, neither would the employees. He would reward individual initiative, but the real gains in salary and bonus would come only if the enterprise as a whole did well. He paid particularly close attention to the big bonuses to be paid to the investment bankers, going through the list one at a time to *ensure that each bonus was earned,* not just awarded.

- He devoted an *intense effort to discovering and managing risk* within JPMorgan Chase's diverse array of businesses. When the board's risk committee held a meeting, he was there. A large part of Dimon's job was simply listening to people, gathering intelligence. That was how he got an early warning from his consumer lending people that mortgages were beginning to become a problem. That warning prompted him to begin substantial withdrawal from the subprime market and the derivative products that would become so deeply toxic in 2008.

Prince's experience as head of CitiGroup was vastly different:

- He *lacked Dimon's operating experience.* Prince's legal background had been highly useful in structuring deals and minimizing the impact of the WorldCom and Enron scandals, but had done little to prepare him to oversee a vast and very complex financial empire.

- He *failed to understand the business and the people.* Sandy Weill had been a savvy people person and had staffed the bank with experts in every area. But Weill created CitiGroup through mergers of very different corporate cultures, such as Salomon Brothers, Smith Barney, Travelers, and the old CitiBank. That resulted in a *fractious culture* in which people and subsidiaries were looking out for themselves, not for the overall well-being of the company.

- He didn't get much-needed advice from senior executives. While former Treasury Secretary Robert Rubin was a highly vaunted adviser to Prince and the CitiGroup board, in retrospect he proved curiously *detached from CitiGroup's operations.* Prince also made a critical mistake when Robert Willumstad, the veteran operating executive who was serving as president of CitiGroup, resigned after being passed over for the chairman's position. Rather than place operations under an experienced operations executive, Prince assumed Willumstad's operating responsibilities.

- Prince understood the legal and reputational risks inherent in scandals like Enron or WorldCom, but he did not understand the business risks from new, exotic financial products.

The stage thus was set for these two financial behemoths to plunge into the biggest and most wrenching financial crisis to hit the big banks since the Great Depression. The strategy, people, and operations at JPMorgan Chase met the challenge. Dimon was even able to take advantage of the crisis to buy up the assets of the failing Bear Stearns and Washington Mutual for pennies on the dollar, expanding his company's scope and market share. CitiGroup, however, was unable to cope as the global financial system teetered on the verge of collapse. The toxic assets on CitiGroup's balance sheet quickly became overwhelming and on November 4, 2007, Prince resigned. He was among the first major financial leaders to be ousted amid the developing crisis. In 2008 *Fortune* magazine named Prince as one of eight economic leaders who failed to see the economic crisis coming. As we write this, CitiGroup is a mere shell of its former self, the victim of poor execution in a time of crisis, while JPMorgan Chase stands poised to emerge from the crisis more powerful than ever.

THE SEVEN ESSENTIAL BEHAVIORS

Just as the three core processes of execution remain essential to getting things done, albeit with some modification to accommodate the global resetting that is occurring, so, too, do the seven essential behaviors. They are fundamental things you must do to execute well, but they must be undertaken in the context of the times. And like the three processes, the seven essential behaviors do not each stand alone, but are linked with one another. We explain them in Chapter 3, but here is a brief explanation about how current circumstances require some modification in how to think about and act on them.

KNOW YOUR PEOPLE AND KNOW YOUR BUSINESS. In *Execution* we stress the need for domain knowledge, the kind of granular understanding of how the business makes money that goes beyond profit and loss statements. We assumed that people who knew their business in that up-close and personal way also knew the risks implicit in that business. We were only half-right. We are all now painfully aware that while many people knew how their business made money, far too few knew the risks that were inherent in how they made that money. Worse, as they competed against companies in the same business, each failed to realize that they were all taking the same risks. The chances of something going wrong may have been relatively small, but because they were all making the same bets, the *consequences* if something did go wrong could be—and, of course, were—calamitous.

While Lehman Brothers failed amid the cascading problems associated with high-leverage and toxic assets, Goldman Sachs survived because it had a much better handle on the risk inherent in its business. Traders were trained in evaluating risk, executives were cross-trained in many aspects of the overall business, and the company's risk managers were highly regarded and well rewarded rather than being seen as obstacles to making even more money as they were at other firms. All of that combined to permit Goldman to identify the turn in the tide and execute internally to cope with it.

There are, of course, many examples of companies that neither understand their own business nor the risks inherent in it. Take Starbucks. For years the company operated on the assumption that it could keep raising prices even in the face of growing competition. Remarkably, it got away with it for years. But eventually reality caught up and it became painfully clear that people feeling pinched financially would find ways to save money. One way to do that was to buy a cheaper cup of coffee from the likes of Dunkin' Donuts or McDonald's. Now, Starbucks is struggling to reset its own business under highly stressful economic conditions. And one need only watch a New York Yankees home game on television to see the tiers of empty seats behind home plate to know that the Yankees' management badly miscalculated the willingness of fans to pay exorbitant prices in a recession, even in the Yankees' spiffy new stadium.

Knowing your people is just as important as knowing your business in these perilous times. Knowing your people obviously requires rigorous evaluation against clear goals and candid and thorough feedback. But it also requires you to become a better listener, seeking peoples' opinions and ideas even when they may not be as forceful in making their points or arguments as others. Listen to your people and learn who among them is grounded in reality, undeterred by obstacles, and determined to execute the strategy come hell or high water. You will also be better able to assess your organization's ability to undertake the radical changes that may be necessary to weather the storm and position the company for the better times ahead. The failure to know your people can lead to disastrous decisions. One of the most memorable of such failures was Circuit City CEO Philip Schoonover's decision in 2007 to fire many of his company's best-paid salespeople in an effort to curb costs. Not surprisingly, the best-paid salespeople were also the best sales people, and their elimination resulted in exactly what one would expect: lower sales. Circuit City went out of business in January 2009.

But knowing your people is not enough. They need to know you. It is absolutely critical during trying times that you as a leader are accessible, that you project a sense of confidence tempered by concern, that you share as much undistorted and unfiltered information as you can, and that you act decisively. Remember that people are constantly searching for indications about their leader's ability to carry them through a raging storm and they will interpret or misinterpret the slightest signals, whether those signals are sent intentionally or mistakenly.

INSIST ON REALISM. The business environment will never be the same again. No one knows how long the downturn will last or what shape the recovery will take, so realism will involve living with a degree of uncertainty. Something will always be happening to change the status quo so taking anything for granted or running your business by "looking in the rearview mirror" are recipes for failure. Andy Grove, the retired CEO of Intel, summed it up best for us with the title of his book: *Only the Paranoid Survive.* Especially in today's environment, people will see an unrealistically rosy view of the future or will disguise the problems confronting your organization. It is far more important to maintain your credibility as a leader by being relentlessly realistic rather than trying to gloss over problems.

Living with uncertainty, though, doesn't mean paralysis. You have to act on your strategy even as you recognize that the strategy will evolve as circumstances evolve. That means gathering ground-level intelligence by being "out there" observing consumer behavior in the marketplace, not simply receiving reports.

Realism also requires you to have a view of the world outside your business and to be prepared to adapt it to reality and make rational judgments about which threats are fundamental to the survival of your business and which will cost you more to fight than you can possibly win. Wal-Mart's business strategy clearly involves low prices. But it became so obsessed with keeping labor costs low that its tough personnel policies wound up hurting both its stock price and its corporate image. Contrast that hostile approach to personnel with Costco's much more harmonious labor relations and reputation as an employer and it becomes clear that Wal-Mart simply wasn't being realistic about what its tough approach could accomplish.

While *understanding* reality is crucial, equally important is communicating it to your people. In part that means, as noted earlier, knowing your people and listening to their concerns. With the Internet, cell phones, instant messaging, and Twitter easily available to everyone, it's inevitable that incorrect, sometimes malicious, information will spread rapidly. So much information is available that it is impossible to respond to all of it. It doesn't help to become defensive, but if you're listening carefully to what people are talking and worrying about, you will be able from time to time—when particularly egregious or harmful rumors are spreading—to stop and say "That just isn't right. Here's the real information."

IDENTIFY CLEAR GOALS AND PRIORITIES. The ability to identify clear goals and priorities is being tested as the world resets. In 2008, for example, the primary goal for many companies became safety and managing for cash. But within that goal was the related one of managing for risk and a shift from previous years in the balance between the short-term and the long-term. Identifying goals requires a level of savvy and expertise to achieve the right balance. That, in turn, requires the realism and the knowledge of the business and the people that constitute the first two of our seven essential behaviors. Choosing the wrong goals can be disastrous. All too often the wrong goals are set because the leader isn't realistic about the ability of the people to achieve them. Articulating the right goals is the first step. The people in the organization then have to execute and that means setting priorities and benchmarks. It isn't enough to say "we need to generate $10 billion in cash." You have to know what parts of the business will generate how much cash, how they will do it (by better managing inventories and receivables, for example), who is accountable, and how to follow through to be sure everyone is doing what they are supposed to be doing.

A fundamental component of setting any goal is understanding the risks inherent in trying to achieve it. There is no reward without risk, but the failure to understand and guard against those risks jeopardizes the ability to reap the reward. Wall Street has shown us that understanding risks is much more than simply devising sophisticated mathematical models. Such models have their uses, but so does common sense. No doubt the Nobel laureates who devised Long-Term Capital Management's mathematical models a decade ago and the rocket scientists who devised, sold, or invested in the toxic collateralized mortgage obligations—CMOs—that nearly brought down the global financial system in 2008 were smart, but they couldn't see the overall risks that were enveloping them. Once the risks are recognized and analyzed, consider a hedging strategy or limiting your participation in an area in which the risks are great. You can't and wouldn't want to hedge everything, but if a risk threatens the survival of the organization, hedging can be a lifesaver.

FOLLOW-THROUGH. Follow-through is a constant and sequential part of execution. It ensures that you have established closure in the dialogue about who will be responsible for what and the specific milestones for measurement. The failure to establish this closure leaves the people who execute a decision or strategy without a clear picture of their role. As events unfold rapidly amid much uncertainty, follow-through becomes a much more intense process. Milestones need to be placed closer together so there is less room for slippage, and information needs to flow faster and in more detail so that everyone knows how the strategy is evolving.

Follow-through is based on knowledge, but there are times, especially now, when follow-through also requires courage. There were people who were apprehensive about the scale of the collateralized mortgage obligations that their companies were generating. They knew that in the wrong circumstances CMOs could create serious problems. Yet there is little evidence that they had the courage to address the issue in the face of the huge amounts of money being minted through the issuance of CMOs and other exotic derivative products. For follow-through to serve its function, action must follow analysis. Knowledge without courage isn't effective.

REWARD THE DOERS. This is a critical part of achieving success that we stressed in *Execution*. In the intervening years, however, the significance and importance of rewarding the doers has led to excessive compensation plans that are severely out of balance. There is no question that these plans became far too biased toward short-term results and often toward the wrong results, i.e., the number of mortgages sold rather than how sound a mortgage was. Companies developed what we call "pay as you go" compensation systems that put a disproportionate emphasis on short-term results. That provided a huge incentive for people to take far more risks than they should have in order to grab the big bonuses. And when all the big banks and investment firms were using essentially the same compensation structures, the global risks spun out of control.

In the run up to the financial crisis of 2008, people in the financial services industry, for example, were being paid to write CMOs with no regard to the long-term performance of these instruments. And the same incentive mind-set permeated the economy from chief executives of major companies like Fannie Mae and Freddie Mac, who garnered huge bonuses despite poor performance, to the storefront offices of mortgage brokers. Mortgage brokers were paid for the number of mortgages they initiated. Those mortgages were then sold, and there were no consequences and thus no regard for how sound those mortgages were.

Of course, to properly reward the "doers" you must correctly define what a doer is. This is central to the idea of execution. Simply put, a doer is a person who gets things done. Doing is meeting goals. Some goals are legitimately short-term goals that yield short-term results and are properly compensated on a short-term basis. But other goals are long-term and by definition we will not know if we have achieved those goals for some time. Consequently the people striving to meet those goals should be compensated on a long-term basis, with some portion of that long-term compensation based on achieving critical milestones toward the goal. And there are some goals that are so long-term that compensation should only be awarded when a person retires and his or her contributions to meeting those extremely long-term goals can be assessed. Leaders must take responsibility for setting the right rewards for doers. This is particularly true of boards of directors, many of which made egregiously bad calls in rewarding poor performance by the CEOs of their companies.

Linked together as these behaviors are, rewarding the doers must be based on the correct metrics. For too long companies—and this often involved boards of directors—set "shareholder value" as one of the goals to be measured and rewarded in compensation plans. But the directors and CEOs who set shareholder value as a goal missed an essential point. Increasing shareholder value is an outcome, not a goal. If you set the right strategy with the right goals and execute well to implement the strategy and achieve the goals—growth in earnings per share, good cash flow, improved market share, for example—then shareholder value is the result. Get everything else right and shareholder value will take care of itself.

EXPAND PEOPLES' CAPABILITIES. The fundamentals of this essential behavior don't change. Even in tough times you can find ways to provide education and training as an investment in the company's future. Even though promotions may be few and far between in this toxic environment, you can still find ways to stretch and test your people. It goes without saying that you need to do precise, accurate, and candid appraisals, but be sure you are looking for the qualities that matter amid the current turmoil: energy, courage, honesty, integrity, and perseverance. You need people who can roll with the punches, not people who are whiners and naysayers. You also need to rethink which people are more likely to rise to the top in the new environment as your organization's strategy evolves. Lou Gerstner did a fine job of reviving IBM's computer business, but he also had the wisdom to look ahead and see that IBM would need to become a more service-oriented company. As a result he cultivated Sam Palmisano, with his extensive service career, to succeed him, a move that demonstrates Gerstner's ability to execute. Palmisano has been adding steadily to IBM's service business, including expanding service capability abroad and entering into partnerships that give the company broader and deeper expertise.

KNOW YOURSELF. This seventh behavior is perhaps the most crucial and applies to every leader, but is especially important for CEOs. When people take the corner office they either grow or swell. Mark Hurd at Hewlett-Packard and Ronald Williams at Aetna are great examples of leaders who are growing in the CEO's job. Dennis Koslowski, the former head of Tyco, merely swelled in the job and went to prison as a result of his misuse of corporate assets. And even those who grow in the job are confronted by "The CEO Is Always Right" syndrome that inadvertently stifles much-needed dissent and argument. Thus you have to rely on yourself to contain your own ego and recognize your inevitable blind spots. Be particularly cautious about losing your ability to listen. Not only do you need expertise from both within and outside the company to shore up your blind spots and weaknesses, but also a pipeline to people willing and able to bring you diverse views and bad news. Above all, you need to be able to recognize when you're part of the problem. We give high marks to Bill Ford, first for taking on the challenge of leading his family's company, then for realizing that the job was too much for him and essentially firing himself to bring in Allan Mulally to try to revive Ford's failing fortunes. As of this writing Ford is surviving without government loans, which is more than can be said for its longtime rivals, General Motors and Chrysler.

THE WAY FORWARD

The ancient Chinese curse—"May you live in interesting times!"—is upon us. How and when we emerge from the economic and financial problems afflicting the globe today is far from certain. Government and business leaders all over the world are in uncharted waters, each trying to find the right way forward. It is a difficult task, but not an impossible one. The leaders who find the right solutions for their own organizations in the changing world that is emerging doubtless will reap the rewards due them.

There are several characteristics that will differentiate good leaders going forward. They will have a commanding knowledge of the world around them. They will never stop learning. They will be extremely flexible and quick to adapt to changing conditions. But perhaps most important of all, they will lead in a positive and uplifting way that gives confidence to those who follow.

Whether you are reading *Execution* for the first time or rereading it for the tenth time, rest assured that the principles of execution are timeless and will provide guidelines to help you make your way. It is only the methodology of applying those principles that changes with changing circumstances.

EXECUTION

INTRODUCTION

LARRY*: My job at Honeywell International these days is to restore the discipline of execution to a company that had lost it. Many people regard execution as detail work that's beneath the dignity of a business leader. That's wrong. To the contrary, it's a leader's most important job.

This particular journey began in 1991 when, after a thirty-four-year career at General Electric, I was named AlliedSignal's CEO. I was accustomed to an organization that got things done, where people met their commitments. I took execution for granted. So it was a shock when I got to AlliedSignal. Sure, I knew it would be in rough shape, but I wasn't prepared for the malaise I found. The company had lots of hardworking, bright peo-

---

*Throughout this book, coauthors Larry Bossidy and Ram Charan will provide insights written in the first person. Larry talks primarily from his experience as a senior executive at General Electric, AlliedSignal, and Honeywell International. Ram speaks from his wide-ranging thirty-five years of experience as an adviser to business leaders and boards of directors around the world.

ple, but they weren't effective, and they didn't place a premium on getting things done.

Viewed on the surface, AlliedSignal had the same basic core processes as GE or most other companies: it had one for people, one for strategy, and one for budgeting or operations. But unlike the processes at GE, those at AlliedSignal weren't yielding results. When you manage these processes in depth, you get robust outputs. You get answers to critical questions: Are our products positioned optimally in the marketplace? Can we identify how we're going to turn the plan into specific results for growth and productivity? Are we staffed with the right kinds of people to execute the plan? If not, what are we going to do about it? How do we make sure the operating plan has sufficiently specific programs to deliver the outcomes to which we've committed?

At AlliedSignal, we weren't even asking those questions. The processes were empty rituals, almost abstractions. People did a lot of work on them, but very little of it was useful. The business unit strategic plans, for example, were six-inch-thick books full of data about products, but the data had little to do with strategy. The operating plan was strictly a numbers exercise, with little attention paid to action plans for growth, markets, productivity, or quality. People were holding the same jobs too long, and many plants were run by accountants instead of production people.

AlliedSignal had no productivity culture. It measured cost-per-man-hour in its plants but had no companywide measure for real productivity growth. It lacked learning or education. Individual businesses were allowed to have their own identities instead of being joined under the AlliedSignal name. I was told, "We've got a chemical culture, an automotive culture, and an aerospace culture, and they don't like each other." "We've got one stock that investors buy," I replied. "We need one brand."

Most fundamentally, the three core processes were disconnected from the everyday realities of the business, and from each other. Leading these processes is the real job of running a business. The leader has to believe in them and be actively involved in them. But the former CEO hadn't been deeply involved with them. He saw his job as buying and selling businesses.

Our new team conducted the processes with rigor and intensity. By the time I retired—after the merger with Honeywell in 1999—we had tripled our operating margins to almost 15 percent, raised our return on equity from just over 10 percent to 28 percent, and delivered an almost ninefold return for shareholders. How did we do it? We created a discipline of execution.

Putting an execution environment in place is hard, but losing it is easy. Less than two years later, the picture had changed again. The company didn't deliver the results investors expected, and the stock price was down. After the proposed merger with GE fell through, Honeywell's board asked me to spend a year getting the company back on track.

Certainly the distraction and uncertainty of the merger effort had taken a toll. Good people had left or were leaving. But the discipline of execution had unraveled. The intensity of the core processes had waned. Honeywell wasn't getting things done.

Before I left the company, for example, we had developed a turbogenerator product that I thought was a very promising entry into the market for standby power. It would be perfect for small businesses such as 7-Eleven stores. On returning, I found the product had been built incorrectly—it was too small for the market and would run only on natural gas, when we needed to offer both oil and gas alternatives. Sales were pathetic. People expected that I'd find some way to salvage the product—after all, I had been the instigator. But when I looked at the situation, I saw it was too far gone. We'd be better off spending the money on something else. So we closed it down.

When a company executes well, its people are not victims of mistakes like this. If Honeywell had had an execution culture, either the turbogenerator would have been built correctly from the outset, or it would have been fixed soon enough to be successful.

And when a company executes well, its people are not brought to their knees by changes in the business environment. After the tragic events of September 11, we had to tear up our aerospace operating plan for 2001. But we put together a new one in ten days. We identified as best we could the shortfalls of revenue, and we decided what we'd have to do to offset them with cost cuts. We also put a team in place to coordinate and ramp up all of our security products, and we reenergized our defense marketing folks.

RAM: There aren't many companies where leaders would produce a new operating plan for a major part of the company in ten days. More often there'd be a lot of talk and off-site conferences but no action. That's one distinction between companies that execute and those that don't.

Too many leaders fool themselves into thinking their companies are well run. They're like the parents in Garrison Keillor's fictional Lake Wobegon, all of whom think their children are above average. Then the top performers at Lake Wobegon High School arrive at the University of Minnesota or Colgate or Princeton and find out they're average or even below average. Similarly, when corporate leaders start understanding how the GEs and Emerson Electrics of this world are run—how superbly they get things done—they discover how far they have to go before they become world class in execution.

In the past businesses got away with poor execution by pleading for patience. "The business environment is tough right now" is one typical excuse; or "Our strategy will take time to produce results." But the business environment is always tough, and success is no longer measured over years. A company can win or lose serious market share before even it realizes what has hit it. Johnson & Johnson, for example, pioneered the stent, a mesh tube that is inserted surgically and is used to support clogged arteries. In 1997 and 1998 it lost 95 percent of the $700 million market it had created to competitors who offered better technology and lower pricing. Only recently has it begun a comeback, introducing new versions with clear performance advantages.

Execution is now tested on a quarterly basis—and not just by the numbers. Securities analysts look to see whether a company is showing progress toward meeting its quarterly goals. If they think it isn't, their downgrades can wipe out billions of dollars in market capitalization.

Most often today the difference between a company and its competitor is the ability to execute. If your competitors are executing better than you are, they're beating you in the here and now, and the financial markets won't wait to see if your elaborate strategy plays out. So leaders who can't execute don't get free runs anymore. Execution is *the* great unaddressed issue in the business world today. Its absence is the single biggest obstacle to success and the cause of most of the disappointments that are mistakenly attributed to other causes.

As an adviser to senior leaders of companies large and small, I often work with a client for ten or more consecutive years. I have the opportunity to observe corporate dynamics over time and to participate directly in them. I first began to identify the problem of execution more than three decades ago, as I observed that strategic plans often did not work out in practice. As I facilitated meetings at the CEO and division levels, I watched and studied, and I saw that leaders placed too much emphasis on what some call high-level strategy, on intellectualizing and philosophizing, and not enough on implementation. People would agree on a project or initiative, and then nothing would come of it. My own nature is to follow through, so when this happened, I'd pick up the phone, call the person in charge, and ask, "What happened?" In time I saw a pattern and realized that execution was a major issue.

Here is the fundamental problem: people think of execution as the tactical side of business, something leaders delegate while they focus on the perceived "bigger" issues. This idea is completely wrong. Execution is not just tactics—it is a discipline and a system. It has to be built into a company's strategy, its goals, and its culture. And the leader of the organization must be deeply engaged in it. He cannot delegate its substance. Many business leaders spend vast amounts of time learning and promulgating the latest management techniques. But their failure to understand and practice execution negates the value of almost all they learn and preach. Such leaders are building houses without foundations.

■ ■ ■

Execution is not only the biggest issue facing business today; it is something nobody has explained satisfactorily.

Other disciplines have no shortage of accumulated knowledge and literature. Strategy? So much thinking has gone into strategy that it's no longer an intellectual challenge. You can rent any strategy you want from a consulting firm. Leadership development? The literature on it is endless. Innovation? Ditto. Nor is there any shortage of tools and techniques that can help leaders get things done—approaches to organization structure and incentive systems, business process design, methodologies for promoting people, guides to culture change.

We talk to many leaders who fall victim to the gap between promises they've made and results their organizations delivered. They frequently tell us they have a problem with accountability—people aren't doing the things they're supposed to do to implement a plan. They desperately want to make changes of some kind, but what do they need to change? They don't know.

So we see a great need for this book. Execution is not just something that does or doesn't get done. Execution is a specific set of behaviors and techniques that companies need to master in order to have competitive advantage. *It is a discipline of its own.* In big companies and small ones, it is the critical discipline for success now.

Execution will help you, as a business leader, to choose a more robust strategy. In fact, you can't craft a worthwhile strategy if you don't at the same time make sure your organization has or can get what's required to execute it, including the right resources and the right people. Leaders in an execution culture design strategies that are more road maps than rigid paths enshrined in fat planning books. That way they can respond quickly when the unexpected happens. Their strategies are designed to be executed.

Execution paces everything. It enables you to see what's

going on in your industry. It's the best means for change and transition—better than culture, better than philosophy. Execution-oriented companies change faster than others because they're closer to the situation.

If your business has to survive difficult times, if it has to make an important shift in response to change—and these days just about every business does—it's far, far more likely to succeed if it's executing well.

Leading for execution is not rocket science. It's very straightforward stuff. The main requirement is that you as a leader have to be deeply and passionately engaged in your organization and honest about its realities with others and yourself.

This is true whether you're running a whole company or your first profit center. Any business leader, at any company or any level, needs to master the discipline of execution. This is the way you establish credibility as a leader. By the time you've finished this book, you'll understand how to do it. Your know-how of the discipline of execution will be a competitive advantage. If you then proceed to put it into action in your business, we know you'll generate better results.

■ ■ ■

In part 1, chapters 1 and 2, we explain the discipline of execution, why it is so important today, and how it can differentiate you from your competitors. Part 2, chapters 3 to 5, shows that execution doesn't just happen. Fundamental building blocks need to be in place, and we identify and describe the most important: the leader's personal priorities, the social software of culture change, and the leader's most important job—selecting and appraising people.

Part 3 is the how-to section of the book. Chapters 6 to 9 discuss the three core processes of people, strategy, and operations. We show what makes them effective, and how the practice of each process is linked to and integrated with the other two.

Chapter 6 covers the people process, which is the most important of the three. Done well, it results in a leadership gene pool that can conceive and shape executable strategies and convert them into operating plans and specific points of accountability.

Chapters 7 and 8 cover the strategy process. We show how effective strategic planning can bring you from conceptual thinking at 50,000 feet down to reality: this process develops a strategy building block by building block, testing its executability. It also links back to the people process. If the strategy proposed and its backup logic are clearly in sync with the realities of the marketplace, the economy, and the competition, then the people process has worked. The right people are in the right jobs. The problem with many so-called strategies is that they're too abstract and shallow, or else they're really operations plans, not strategies. The leadership and its capabilities may be mismatched: for example, a leader may have great skills in a business function like marketing or finance but may not be a strategist.

In chapter 9 we show that no strategy delivers results unless it's converted into specific actions. The operations process shows how to build, block by block, an operating plan that will deliver the strategy. Both the strategy and operations plans link with the people process to test the match between organizational capabilities and what is required to execute the operating plan.

PART I

WHY EXECUTION IS NEEDED

CHAPTER 1

The Gap Nobody Knows

The CEO was sitting in his office late one evening, looking tired and drained. He was trying to explain to a visitor why his great strategic initiative had failed, but he couldn't figure out what had gone wrong.

"I'm so frustrated," he said. "I got the group together a year ago, people from all the divisions. We had two off-site meetings, did benchmarking, got the metrics. McKinsey helped us. Everybody agreed with the plan. It was a good one, and the market was good.

"This was the brightest team in the industry, no question about it. I assigned stretch goals. I empowered them—gave them the freedom to do what they needed to do. Everybody knew what had to be done. Our incentive system is clear, so they knew what the rewards and penalties would be. We worked together with high energy. How could we fail?

"Yet the year has come to an end, and we missed the goals. They let me down; they didn't deliver the results. I have lowered earnings estimates four times in the past nine months. We've lost our credibility with the Street. I have probably lost my credibility with the board. I don't know what to do, and I don't know where the bottom is. Frankly, I think the board may fire me."

Several weeks later the board did indeed fire him.

This story—it's a true one—is the archetypal story of the gap that nobody knows. It's symptomatic of the biggest problem facing corporations today. We hear lots of similar stories when we talk to business leaders. They're played out almost daily in the press, when it reports on companies that should be succeeding but aren't: Aetna, AT&T, British Airways, Campbell Soup, Compaq, Gillette, Hewlett-Packard, Kodak, Lucent Technologies, Motorola, Xerox, and many others.

These are good companies. They have smart CEOs and talented people, they have inspiring visions, and they bring in the best consultants. Yet they, and many other companies as well, regularly fail to produce promised results. Then when they announce the shortfall, investors dump their stocks and enormous market value is obliterated. Managers and employees are demoralized. And increasingly, boards are forced to dump the CEOs.

The leaders of all the companies listed above were highly regarded when they were appointed—they seemed to have all of the right qualifications. But they all lost their jobs because they didn't deliver what they said they would. In the year 2000 alone, forty CEOs of the top two hundred companies on *Fortune*'s 500 list were removed—not retired but fired or made to resign. When 20 percent of the most powerful business leaders in America lose their jobs, something is clearly wrong. This trend continued in 2001 and will clearly be in evidence in 2002.

In such cases it's not just the CEO who suffers—so do

the employees, alliance partners, shareholders, and even customers. And it's not just the CEO whose shortcomings create the problem, though of course he or she is ultimately responsible.

What is the problem? Is it a rough business environment? Yes. Whether the economy is strong or weak, competition is fiercer than ever. Change comes faster than ever. Investors—who were passive when today's senior leaders started their careers—have turned unforgiving. But this factor by itself doesn't explain the near-epidemic of shortfalls and failures. Despite this, there are companies that deliver on their commitments year in and year out—companies such as GE, Wal-Mart, Emerson, Southwest Airlines, and Colgate-Palmolive.

When companies fail to deliver on their promises, the most frequent explanation is that the CEO's strategy was wrong. But the strategy by itself is not often the cause. Strategies most often fail because they aren't executed well. Things that are supposed to happen don't happen. Either the organizations aren't capable of making them happen, or the leaders of the business misjudge the challenges their companies face in the business environment, or both.

Former Compaq CEO Eckhard Pfeiffer had an ambitious strategy, and he almost pulled it off. Before any of his competitors, he saw that the so-called Wintel architecture—the combination of the Windows operating system and Intel's constant innovation—would serve for everything from a palm-held to a linked network of servers capable of competing with mainframes.

Mirroring IBM, Pfeiffer broadened his base to serve all the computing needs of enterprise customers. He bought Tandem, the high-speed, failsafe mainframe manufacturer, and Digital Equipment Company (DEC) to give Compaq serious entry into the services segment. Pfeiffer moved at breakneck speed on his bold strategic vision, transforming Compaq from a failing niche builder of high-priced office PCs to the second-biggest computer company (after IBM) in just six years. By 1998 it was poised to dominate the industry.

But the strategy looks like a pipe dream today. Integrating the acquisitions and delivering on the promises required better execution than Compaq was able to achieve. More fundamentally, neither Pfeiffer nor his successor, Michael Capellas, pursued the kind of execution necessary to make money as PCs became more and more of a commodity business.

Michael Dell understood that kind of execution. His direct-sales and build-to-order approach was not just a marketing tactic to bypass retailers; it was the core of his business strategy. Execution is the reason Dell passed Compaq in market value years ago, despite Compaq's vastly greater size and scope, and it's the reason Dell passed Compaq in 2001 as the world's biggest maker of PCs. As of November 2001, Dell was shooting to double its market share, from approximately 20 to 40 percent.

Any company that sells direct has certain advantages: control over pricing, no retail markups, and a sales force dedicated to its own products. But that wasn't Dell's secret. After all, Gateway sells direct too, but lately it has fared no better than Dell's other rivals. Dell's insight was that building to order, executing superbly, and keeping a sharp eye on costs would give him an unbeatable advantage.

In conventional batch production manufacturing, a business sets its production volume based on the demand that is forecast for the coming months. If it has outsourced component manufacturing and just does the assembling, like a computer maker, it tells the component suppliers what volumes to expect and negotiates the prices. If sales fall short of projections, everybody gets stuck with unsold inventory. If sales are higher, they scramble inefficiently to meet demand.

Building to order, by contrast, means producing a unit after the customer's order is transmitted to the factory. Component suppliers, who also build to order, get the information when Dell's customers place their orders. They deliver the parts to Dell, which immediately places them into production, and shippers cart away the machines within hours after they're boxed. The system squeezes time out of the entire cycle from order to delivery—Dell can deliver a computer within a week or less of the time an order is placed. This system minimizes inventories at both ends of the pipeline, incoming and outgoing. It also allows Dell customers to get the latest technological improvements more often than rivals' customers.

Build-to-order improves inventory turnover, which increases asset velocity, one of the most underappreciated components of making money. Velocity is the ratio of sales dollars to net assets deployed in the business, which in the most common definition includes plant and equipment, inventories, and accounts receivable minus accounts payable. Higher velocity improves productivity and reduces working capital. It also improves cash flow, the life blood of any business, and can help improve margins as well as revenue and market share.

Inventory turns are especially important for makers of PCs, since inventories account for the largest portion of their net assets. When sales fall below forecast, companies with traditional batch manufacturing, like Compaq, are stuck with unsold inventory. What's more, computer components such as microprocessors are particularly prone to obsolescence because performance advances so rapidly, often accompanied by falling prices. When these PC makers have to write off the excess or obsolete inventory, their profit margins can shrink to the vanishing point.

Dell turns its inventory over eighty times a year, compared with about ten to twenty times for its rivals, and its working capital is negative. As a result, it generates an enormous amount of cash. In the fourth quarter of fiscal 2002, with revenues of $8.1 billion and an operating margin of 7.4 percent, Dell had cash flow of $1 billion from operations. Its return on invested capital for fiscal 2001 was 355 percent—an incredible rate for a company with its sales volume. Its high velocity also allows it to give customers the latest technological improvements ahead of other makers, and to take advantage of falling component costs—either to improve margins or to cut prices.

These are the reasons Dell's strategy became deadly for its competitors once PC growth slowed. Dell capitalized on their misery and cut prices in a bid for market share, increasing the distance between it and the rest of the industry. Because of its high velocity, Dell could show high return on capital and positive cash flow, even with margins depressed. Its competition couldn't.

The system works only because Dell executes meticulously at every stage. The electronic linkages among suppliers and manufacturing create a seamless extended enterprise. A manufacturing executive we know who worked at Dell for a time calls its system "the best manufacturing operation I've ever seen."

As this book goes to press, the merger between Compaq and Hewlett-Packard, proposed in mid-2001, is still up in the air. No matter: Alone or in combination, nothing they do will make them competitive with Dell unless they come up with an equal or better build-to-order production model.

The chronic underperformers we've mentioned so far

have lots of company. Countless others are less than they could be because of poor execution. The gap between promises and results is widespread and clear. The gap nobody knows is the gap between what a company's leaders want to achieve and the ability of their organization to achieve it.

Everybody talks about change. In recent years, a small industry of changemeisters has preached revolution, reinvention, quantum change, breakthrough thinking, audacious goals, learning organizations, and the like. We're not necessarily debunking this stuff. But unless you translate big thoughts into concrete steps for action, they're pointless. Without execution, the breakthrough thinking breaks down, learning adds no value, people don't meet their stretch goals, and the revolution stops dead in its tracks. What you get is change for the worse, because failure drains the energy from your organization. Repeated failure destroys it.

These days we're hearing a more practical phrase on the lips of business leaders. They're talking about taking their organizations to the "next level," which brings the rhetoric down to earth. GE CEO Jeff Immelt, for example, is asking his people how they can use technology to differentiate their way to the next level and command better prices, margins, and revenue growth.

This is an execution approach to change. It's reality-based—people can envision and discuss specific things they need to do. It recognizes that meaningful change comes only with execution.

No company can deliver on its commitments or adapt well to change unless all leaders practice the discipline of execution at all levels. Execution has to be a part of a company's strategy and its goals. It is the missing link between aspirations and results. As such, it is a major—

indeed, *the* major—job of a business leader. If you don't know how to execute, the whole of your effort as a leader will always be less than the sum of its parts.

EXECUTION COMES OF AGE

Business leaders are beginning to make the connection between execution and results. After Compaq's board fired Pfeiffer, chairman and founder Ben Rosen took pains to say that the company's strategy was fine. The change, he said, would be "in execution. . . . Our plans are to speed up decision-making and make the company more efficient." When Lucent's board dismissed CEO Richard McGinn in October 2000, his replacement, Henry Schacht, explained: "Our issues are ones of execution and focus."

Clients of high-level headhunters are calling and saying, "Find me a guy who can execute." Writing in IBM's 2000 annual report, Louis V. Gerstner said of Samuel Palmisano, the man who would succeed him, "His real expertise is making sure we execute well." Early in 2001 the National Association of Corporate Directors added "execution" to the list of items that directors need to focus on in evaluating their own performance. Directors, the group says, have to ask themselves how well the company is executing and what accounts for any gap between expectations and management's performance. Very few boards now ask these questions, the group noted.

But for all the talk about execution, hardly anybody knows what it is. When we're teaching about execution, we first ask people to define it. They think they know how, and they usually start out well enough. "It's about getting things done," they'll say. "It's about running the company, versus conceiving and planning. It's making our goals." Then we ask them *how* to get things done, and the dialogue goes rapidly downhill. Whether they're students or senior executives, it is soon clear—to them as well as to us—that they don't have the foggiest idea of what it means to execute.

It's no different when execution is mentioned in books, newspapers, or magazines. You get the impression (implicitly), that it's about doing things more effectively, more carefully, with more attention to the details. But nobody really spells out what they mean.

Even people who pinpoint execution as the cause of failure tend to think of it in terms of attention to detail. Ben Rosen used the right word in his remarks, for example, but if he understood what execution actually requires, Compaq's leadership never got the message.

To understand execution, you have to keep three key points in mind:

- *Execution is a discipline, and integral to strategy.*
- *Execution is the major job of the business leader.*
- *Execution must be a core element of an organization's culture.*

Execution Is a Discipline

People think of execution as the tactical side of business. That's the first big mistake. Tactics are central to execution, but execution is not tactics. Execution is fundamental to strategy and has to shape it. No worthwhile strategy can be planned without taking into account the organization's ability to execute it. If you're talking about the smaller specifics of getting things done, call the process

21

implementation, or sweating the details, or whatever you want to. But don't confuse execution with tactics.

Execution is a systematic process of rigorously discussing hows and whats, questioning, tenaciously following through, and ensuring accountability. It includes making assumptions about the business environment, assessing the organization's capabilities, linking strategy to operations and the people who are going to implement the strategy, synchronizing those people and their various disciplines, and linking rewards to outcomes. It also includes mechanisms for changing assumptions as the environment changes and upgrading the company's capabilities to meet the challenges of an ambitious strategy.

In its most fundamental sense, execution is a systematic way of exposing reality and acting on it. Most companies don't face reality very well. As we shall see, that's the basic reason they can't execute. Much has been written about Jack Welch's style of management—especially his toughness and bluntness, which some people call ruthlessness. We would argue that the core of his management legacy is that he forced realism into all of GE's management processes, making it a model of an execution culture.

The heart of execution lies in the three core processes: the people process, the strategy process, and the operations process. Every business and company uses these processes in one form or the other. But more often than not they stand apart from one another like silos. People perform them by rote and as quickly as possible, so they can get back to their perceived work. Typically the CEO and his senior leadership team allot less than half a day each year to review the plans—people, strategy, and operations. Typically too the reviews are not particularly interactive. People sit passively watching PowerPoint presentations. They don't ask questions.

They don't debate, and as a result they don't get much useful outcome. People leave with no commitments to the action plans they've helped create. This is a formula for failure. You need robust dialogue to surface the realities of the business. You need accountability for results—discussed openly and agreed to by those responsible—to get things done and reward the best performers. You need follow-through to ensure the plans are on track.

These processes are where the things that matter about execution need to be decided. Businesses that execute, as we shall see, prosecute them with rigor, intensity, and depth. Which people will do the job, and how will they be judged and held accountable? What human, technical, production, and financial resources are needed to execute the strategy? Will the organization have the ones it needs two years out, when the strategy goes to the next level? Does the strategy deliver the earnings required for success? Can it be broken down into doable initiatives? People engaged in the processes argue these questions, search out reality, and reach specific and practical conclusions. Everybody agrees about their responsibilities for getting things done, and everybody commits to those responsibilities.

The processes are also tightly linked with one another, not compartmentalized among staffs. Strategy takes account of people and operational realities. People are chosen and promoted in light of strategic and operational plans. Operations are linked to strategic goals and human capacities.

Most important, the leader of the business and his or her leadership team are deeply engaged in all three. *They* are the owners of the processes—not the strategic planners or the human resources (HR) or finance staffs.

Execution Is the Job of the Business Leader

Lots of business leaders like to think that the top dog is exempt from the details of actually running things. It's a pleasant way to view leadership: you stand on the mountaintop, thinking strategically and attempting to inspire your people with visions, while managers do the grunt work. This idea creates a lot of aspirations for leadership, naturally. Who wouldn't want to have all the fun and glory while keeping their hands clean? Conversely, who wants to tell people at a cocktail party, "My goal is to be a manager," in an era when the term has become almost pejorative?

This way of thinking is a fallacy, one that creates immense damage.

An organization can execute only if the leader's heart and soul are immersed in the company. Leading is more than thinking big, or schmoozing with investors and lawmakers, although those are part of the job. The leader has to be engaged personally and deeply in the business. Execution requires a comprehensive understanding of a business, its people, and its environment. The leader is the only person in a position to achieve that understanding. And only the leader can make execution happen, through his or her deep personal involvement in the substance and even the details of execution.

The leader must be in charge of getting things done by running the three core processes—picking other leaders, setting the strategic direction, and conducting operations. These actions are the substance of execution, and leaders cannot delegate them regardless of the size of the organization.

How good would a sports team be if the coach spent all his time in his office making deals for new players, while delegating actual coaching to an assistant? A coach is effective because he's constantly observing players individually and collectively on the field and in the locker room. That's how he gets to know his players and their capabilities, and how they get firsthand the benefit of his experience, wisdom, and expert feedback.

It's no different for a business leader. Only a leader can ask the tough questions that everyone needs to answer, then manage the process of debating the information and making the right trade-offs. And only the leader who's intimately engaged in the business can know enough to have the comprehensive view and ask the tough incisive questions.

Only the leader can set the tone of the dialogue in the organization. Dialogue is the core of culture and the basic unit of work. How people talk to each other absolutely determines how well the organization will function. Is the dialogue stilted, politicized, fragmented, and butt-covering? Or is it candid and reality-based, raising the right questions, debating them, and finding realistic solutions? If it's the former—as it is in all too many companies—reality will never come to the surface. If it is to be the latter, the leader has to be on the playing field with his management team, practicing it consistently and forcefully.

Specifically, the leader has to run the three core processes and has to run them with intensity and rigor.

LARRY: When I appoint a new business manager, I call her into the office to discuss three issues. First, she is to behave with the highest integrity. This is an issue where there are no second chances—breach the rule, and you're out. Second, she must know that the customer comes first. And finally I say, "You've got to understand the three processes, for people, strategy, and operations, and you've got to manage these three processes. The more intensity and focus you put on them, the better you make this place. If you don't understand that, you've got no chance of succeeding here."

Companies that do these processes in depth fare dramatically better than those that just *think* they do. If your company doesn't do them in depth, you aren't getting what you deserve out of them. You put in a lot of time and effort and don't get useful output.

For example, everyone likes to say that people are the most important ingredient in their success. But they often hand off the job of assessing people and rewarding them to the HR staff, then rubber-stamp the recommendations at their reviews. Far too many leaders avoid debating about people openly in group settings. That's no way to lead. Only line leaders who know the people can make the right judgments. Good judgments come from practice and experience.

When things are running well, I spend 20 percent of my time on the people process. When I'm rebuilding an organization, it's 40 percent. I'm not talking about doing formal interviews or selecting staff; I mean really getting to know people. When I go out to visit a plant, I'll sit down for the first half hour with the manager. We'll have a discussion about the capability of his people, looking at who is performing well and who needs help. I'll go to a meeting of the whole staff and listen to what they have to say. Then I'll sit down after the meeting and talk about my impressions of the people and write a letter confirming the agreements made at the meeting. And I'll assess people's performance not just at our formal reviews but two or three times a year.

When we were putting these processes into place at

AlliedSignal, one guy—a pretty good guy—said to me at a meeting, "You know, I've got to go through this people ritual again this year." I said, "That's the dumbest comment I've ever heard, because you tell the world how little you know about your job. If you really feel that way, you've got to do something else, because if you're not going to get good at this, you can't be successful." I didn't say it in front of everybody, but I thought to myself, *That just tells me maybe I've got the wrong guy.*

But he didn't do that again. I don't think he ever came to love the people process, but he did it, and he got something out of it. He got to know his staff and made it better.

■ ■ ■

Leaders often bristle when we say they have to run the three core processes themselves. "You're telling me to micromanage my people, and I don't do that," is a common response. Or, "It's not my style. I'm a hands-off leader. I delegate, I empower."

We agree completely that micromanaging is a big mistake. It diminishes people's self-confidence, saps their initiative, and stifles their ability to think for themselves. It's also a recipe for screwing things up—micromanagers rarely know as much about what needs to be done as the people they're harassing, the ones who actually do it.

But there's an enormous difference between leading an organization and presiding over it. The leader who boasts of her hands-off style or puts her faith in empowerment is not dealing with the issues of the day. She is not confronting the people responsible for poor performance, or searching for problems to solve and then making sure they get solved. She is presiding, and she's only doing half her job.

Leading for execution is not about micromanaging, or being "hands-on," or disempowering people. Rather, it's about active involvement—doing the things leaders should be doing in the first place. As you read on, you'll see how leaders who excel at execution immerse themselves in the substance of execution and even some of the key details. They use their knowledge of the business to constantly probe and question. They bring weaknesses to light and rally their people to correct them.

The leader who executes assembles an architecture of execution. He puts in place a culture and processes for executing, promoting people who get things done more quickly and giving them greater rewards. His personal involvement in that architecture is to assign the tasks and then follow up. This means making sure that people understand the priorities, which are based on his comprehensive understanding of the business, and asking incisive questions. The leader who executes often does not even have to tell people what to do; she asks questions so they can figure out what they need to do. In this way she coaches them, passing on her experience as a leader and educating them to think in ways they never thought before. Far from stifling people, this kind of leadership helps them expand their own capabilities for leading.

Jack Welch, Sam Walton, and Herb Kelleher of Southwest Airlines were powerful presences in their organizations. Just about everybody knew them, knew what they stood for, and knew what they expected of their people. Was it because of their forceful personalities? Yes, but a forceful personality doesn't mean anything by itself.

"Chainsaw Al" Dunlap, the celebrated and outspoken champion of savage cost-cutting, had a forceful personality—and he wrecked the companies he was supposedly turning around.

Are leaders like Jack, Sam, and Herb good communicators? Again: yes, but. Communication can be mere boilerplate, or it can mean something. What counts is the substance of the communication and the nature of the person doing the communicating—including his or her ability to listen as well as to talk.

Maybe such people are good leaders because they practice "management by walking around." We've all read the stories about Herb or Sam popping up on the front lines to chat with baggage handlers or stockroom clerks. Sure, walking around is useful and important—but only if the leader doing the walking knows what to say and what to listen for.

Leaders of this ilk are powerful and influential presences because they *are* their businesses. They are intimately and intensely involved with their people and operations. They connect because they know the realities and talk about them. They're knowledgeable about the details. They're excited about what they're doing. They're passionate about getting results. This is not "inspiration" through exhortation or speechmaking. These leaders energize everyone by the example they set.

In his last year as GE's CEO, Jack Welch—as he had done for twenty years in the job—spent a week of ten-hour days reviewing the operating plans of the company's various units. He was intimately involved in the back-and-forth dialogue. Even at the end of his career, Jack wasn't presiding. He was leading by being actively involved.

Execution Has to Be in the Culture

It should be clear by now that execution isn't a program you graft onto your organization. A leader who says, "Okay, now we're going to execute for a change" is merely launching another fad of the month, with no staying power. Just as the leader has to be personally involved in execution, so must everyone else in the organization understand and practice the discipline.

Execution has to be embedded in the reward systems and in the norms of behavior that everyone practices. Indeed, as we will show in chapter 4, focusing on execution is not only an essential part of a business's culture, it is the one sure way to create meaningful cultural change.

One way to get a handle on execution is to think of it as akin to the Six Sigma processes for continual improvement. People practicing this methodology look for deviations from desired tolerances. When they find them, they move quickly to correct the problem. They use the processes to constantly raise the bar, improving quality and throughput. They use them collaboratively across units to improve how processes work across the organization. It's a relentless pursuit of reality, coupled with processes for constant improvement. And it's a huge change in behavior—a change, really, in culture.

Leaders who execute look for deviations from desired managerial tolerances—the gap between the desired and actual outcome in everything from profit margins to the selection of people for promotion. Then they move to close the gap and raise the bar still higher across the whole organization. Like Six Sigma, the discipline of execution doesn't work unless people are schooled in it and practice it constantly; it doesn't work if only a few people in the system practice it. Execution has to be part of an organization's culture, driving the behavior of all leaders at all levels.

Execution should begin with the senior leaders, but if you are not a senior leader, you can still practice it in your own organization. You build and demonstrate your own skills. The results will advance your career—and they may just persuade others in the business to do the same.

WHY PEOPLE DON'T GET IT

If execution is so important, why is it so neglected? To be sure, people in business aren't totally oblivious to it. But what they're mostly aware of is its absence. They know, deep down, that something is missing when decisions don't get made or followed through and when commitments don't get met. They search and struggle for answers, benchmarking companies that are known to deliver on their commitments, looking for the answers in the organizational structure or processes or culture. But they rarely apprehend the underlying lesson, because execution hasn't yet been recognized or taught as a discipline. They literally don't know what they're looking for.

The real problem is that *execution* just doesn't sound very sexy. It's the stuff a leader delegates. Do great CEOs and Nobel Prize winners achieve their glory through execution? Well, yes, in fact, and therein lies the grand fallacy.

The common view of intellectual challenge is only half true. What most people miss today is that intellectual challenge also includes the rigorous and tenacious work of developing and proving the ideas. Perhaps it's the result of the TV generation's upbringing, believing a mythology in which ideas develop instantly into full-blown outcomes.

31

There are different kinds of intellectual challenges. Conceiving a grand idea or broad picture is usually intuitive. Shaping the broad picture into a set of executable actions is analytical, and it's a huge intellectual, emotional, and creative challenge.

Nobel Prize winners succeed because they execute the details of a proof that other people can replicate, verify, or do something with. They test and discover patterns, connections, and linkages that nobody saw before. It took Albert Einstein more than a decade to develop the detailed proof explaining the theory of relativity. That was the execution—the details of proof in mathematical calculations. The theorem would not have been valid without the proof. Einstein could not have delegated this execution. It was an intellectual challenge that nobody else could meet.

The intellectual challenge of execution is in getting to the heart of an issue through persistent and constructive probing. Let's say a manager in the X division plans an 8 percent sales increase in the coming year, even though the market is flat. In their budget reviews, most leaders would accept the number without debate or discussion. But in an execution company's operating review, the leader will want to know if the goal is realistic. "Fine," she'll ask the manager, "but where will the increase come from? What products will generate the growth? Who will buy them, and what pitch are we going to develop for those customers? What will our competitor's reaction be? What will our milestones be?" If a milestone hasn't been reached at the end of the first quarter, it's a yellow light: something's not going as planned, and something will need to be changed.

If the leader has doubts about the organization's capacity to execute, she may drill down even further. "Are the right people in charge of getting it done," she may ask, "and is their accountability clear? Whose collaboration will be required, and how will they be motivated to collaborate? Will the reward system motivate them to a common objective?" In other words, the leader doesn't just sign off on a plan. She wants an explanation, and she will drill down until the answers are clear. Her leadership skills are such that everyone present is engaged in the dialogue, bringing everyone's viewpoint out into the open and assessing the degree and nature of buy-in. It's not simply an opportunity for her managers to learn from her and she from them; it's a way to diffuse the knowledge to everyone in the plan.

Suppose the issue is how to increase productivity. Other questions will be asked: "We have five programs in the budget, and you say we're going to save at least a couple million dollars on each one. What are the programs? Where is the money going to be saved? What's the timeline? How much is it going to cost us to achieve it? And who is responsible for it all?"

■ ■ ■

Organizations don't execute unless the right people, individually and collectively, focus on the right details at the right time. For you as a leader, moving from the concept to the critical details is a long journey. You have to review a wide array of facts and ideas, the permutations and combinations of which can approach infinity. You have to discuss what risks to take, and where. You have to thread through these details, selecting those that count. You have to assign them to the people who matter, and make sure which key ones must synchronize their work.

Such decision making requires knowledge of the business and the external environment. It requires the ability to make fine judgments about people—their capabilities, their reliability, their strengths, and their weaknesses. It requires intense focus and incisive thinking. It requires superb skills in conducting candid, realistic dialogue. This work is as intellectually challenging as any we know of.

Leadership without the discipline of execution is incomplete and ineffective. Without the ability to execute, all other attributes of leadership become hollow. In chapter 2 we demonstrate, through the stories of four businesses and their leaders, why execution makes all the difference in the world.

CHAPTER 2

The Execution Difference

Every great leader has had an instinct for execution. He has said, in effect, "Unless I can make this plan *happen*, it's not going to matter." But the selection, training, and development of leaders doesn't focus on this reality. Judging from our observations, a high proportion of those who actually rise to the top of a business organization have made their mark—their personal "brand"— as high-level thinkers. They are the kind of people who get caught up in the intellectual excitement of each new big idea that comes out and adopt it with enthusiasm. They are articulate conceptualizers, very good at grasping strategies and explaining them. This, they know, is what it takes to get ahead. They aren't interested in the "how" of getting things done; that's for somebody else to think about.

Judging a person's intelligence is easy for people who hire and promote others; it's harder to research a person's track record and gauge their know-how about getting things done, particularly when the performance is the result of many people working together. But the intelligent, articulate conceptualizers don't necessarily understand how to execute. Many don't realize what needs to be done to convert a vision into specific tasks, because their high-level thinking is too broad. They don't follow through and get things done; the details bore them. They don't crystallize thought or anticipate roadblocks. They don't know how to pick people for their organizations who can execute. Their lack of engagement deprives them of the sound judgment about people that comes only through practice.

THE TROUBLE WITH JOE

Joe, the CEO whose downfall we described in chapter 1, is a typical leader who didn't know how to execute. Let's take a closer look at his story, along with those of two prominent CEOs whose companies failed to execute the leaders' grand visions.

You'll recall that Joe couldn't understand why his people hadn't delivered the anticipated results. He'd brought in a top consulting firm to design a new strategy. He made several acquisitions and had a great relationship with Wall Street. Based on his deal-making skills and acquisitions, the company's price/earnings ratio shot up in less than two years. Joe's strength lay in marketing and customer contacts, but he also had a good, close relationship with his CFO. Joe set stretch goals, and the CFO handed the numbers down to the operating people. No micromanager, Joe left the details of implementation to his direct reports, including the executive vice president for the North American business unit and his director of production. But Joe stayed on top of the quarterly numbers. If they came up short, he was on the phone immediately with the people in charge, telling them in the strongest terms possible that they needed to shape up. The quarterly reviews were less than civil.

By the standards of conventional management analysis, Joe did all the right things. By the standards of execution, he did almost nothing right. The gap between goals and outcome reflected a chasm between Joe's ambitions and the realities of the organization. In fact, the goals he set had been unrealistic from day one.

A major problem was that the company's plant could not build enough of the product because its managers were 12 months behind schedule in implementing a process-improvement plan that was 12 months behind schedule. Joe didn't know that. Though he chewed his executives out when they didn't make their numbers, he never asked *why* they didn't make them. An execution-savvy leader would have asked that right away. Then he would have focused on the cause—after all, you don't fix a problem just by looking at its outcome. Was the installation of the process on schedule? he would have asked. Did the executive vice president and his director of operations know the reasons, and what are they doing about it?

Like many CEOs, Joe believed it was the production director's job to ask such questions, and the executive vice president's job to make sure they were asked. But (again, like many CEOs) Joe hadn't picked the right people for the right jobs. Neither man was much on execution. The executive vice president was a ticket puncher who moved almost every three years from one job to another. The production director was a highly intelligent finance guy who came from a consulting firm and was regarded as a "hi-po"—a high-potential candidate to succeed the CEO in five years. But he didn't understand operations at all and was acerbic. The plant managers reporting to him didn't respect him.

If the leaders had had an open dialogue with the manufacturing people, they might have learned about the manufacturing obstacle, but that wasn't in their makeup. They just handed the numbers down. Furthermore, while stretch goals can be useful in forcing people to break old rules and do things better, they're worse than useless if they're totally unrealistic, or if the people who have to meet them aren't given the chance to debate them beforehand and take ownership of them.

How would Joe have behaved differently if he had had the know-how of execution? First, he would have involved all the people responsible for the strategic plan's outcome—including the key production people—in shaping the plan. They would have set goals based on the organization's capability for delivering results. Organizational capability includes having the right people in the right jobs. If the executive vice president didn't know how to get things done, Joe would long ago have coached him on what he needed to do and helped him learn how to execute. If he still wasn't making progress, the only option left would have been to replace him (as the new CEO who took over did). Second, Joe would also have asked his people about the *hows* of execution: how, specifically, were they going to achieve their projected demand on a timely basis, their inventory turns, and cost and quality goals? Anybody who didn't have the answers would have to get them before the plan was launched.

Third, Joe would have set milestones for the progress of the plan, with strict accountability for the people in charge. If they were installing a new process to improve yields, for example, Joe would have made an agreement with them that the project would be X percent completed by Y date, and that Z percent of the people would be . trained in the process. If the managers couldn't meet the milestones, they would have told him, and he would have helped them take corrective actions. Fourth, Joe would have set contingency plans to deal with the unexpected— a shift in the market, say, or a component shortage, or some other change in the external environment.

Joe was very bright but he didn't know how to execute. The people who hired him saw nothing in his record to indicate he'd fail—because they did not use execution as a selection criterion. His reputation for deal making and for making savvy acquisitions had earned him the job.

When the board fired him, it brought in a management team that knew how to execute. The new CEO came from manufacturing. He and his team reviewed and discussed the hows with plant managers, set milestones, and followed through with discipline and consistency to review them.

THE EXECUTION GAP AT XEROX

The people at Xerox who hired Richard C. Thoman saw no reason why he'd fail either. Thoman was one of the most thoughtful people to head a major American company in recent years, and a highly respected strategist. When Xerox hired him as COO in 1997, he was one of Louis V. Gerstner's protégés at IBM, where he'd been CFO. Thoman was brought in to bring change. While COO, he launched numerous cost-cutting initiatives, including layoffs and cuts in bonuses, travel, and perks. He also laid the groundwork for a new strategy. After the board elevated him to CEO in April 1999, he set out to transform Xerox from a products and services company into a solutions provider, combining software, hardware, and services to help customers integrate their paper documents and electronic information flows, organizing partnerships with companies such as Microsoft and Compaq to build the systems.

It was a stirring vision for a company that badly needed one. At the 1999 annual meeting, Thoman told stockholders the company was "poised on the threshold of another period of great success," and predicted that earnings for the year would grow in the mid- to high teens. Investors shared the optimism, bidding the stock price up to record highs.

But the vision was disconnected from reality. Execution had been a problem for decades, and Thoman bit off more than Xerox could chew. For example, in an early step in the company's efforts to refocus itself, he launched two mission-critical initiatives, both of which were gut-wrenching. One aimed to consolidate the company's ninety-some administration centers, which handle accounting, billing, and customer service scheduling and calls, into four. The second would reorganize Xerox's roughly 30,000-person sales force, shifting about half from a geographical focus to an industry focus.

Both moves were necessary and important. The administrative consolidation would cut costs and improve efficiency, and the sales reorganization would pave the way for the intense focus on providing customers with solutions, not just hardware—the core of the new strategy. But by the end of the year, Xerox was in chaos.

In the administrative transition, invoices languished, orders got lost, and service calls went unanswered. Sales representatives had to spend much of their time straightening out the mess, just as they were trying to adapt to a new organization and new way of selling. They also had to build new relationships with customers, since so many had been reassigned to new ones—which, not incidentally, alienated many customers who had been loyal for years.

Morale dropped. Cash flow from operations went negative, and investors began to worry about Xerox's financial viability. The stock price plunged from the sixty-four-dollar range to seven dollars. The company was forced to sell some of its business to meet cash needs. In May 2000, Thoman was summoned to Chairman Paul Allaire's office and told he was out of the job.

What went wrong? While launching two such enormous initiatives at the same time was an execution error—either one alone would have placed a strain on the organization—the problems ran deeper. Thoman's critics argued that he was too aloof to connect with the people who had to execute the changes. But Xerox's clubby culture did not take kindly to an outsider, and as Thoman has pointed out, he did not have the authority to appoint his own leadership team. Especially when a business is making major changes, the right people have to be in the critical jobs, and the core processes must be strong enough to ensure that resistance is dissolved and plans get executed. Both of these building blocks were missing.

OUT OF TOUCH AT LUCENT

Hopes were high when Lucent Technologies named Richard McGinn a CEO in 1996. A strong marketer, McGinn was personable and adept at explaining the company's bright prospects to the investment community. He promised investors dazzling growth in revenues and earnings. Given the climate of the times and seen from an altitude of 50,000 feet, the promises looked credible to the board and to investors. The combination of Western Electric and Bell Labs spun out of AT&T, Lucent would in 1997 concentrate on the booming telecommunications equipment market, from consumer telephones to network switching and transmission gear. With Bell Labs, it had an R&D resource that nobody else could match.

But McGinn had difficulty getting things done inside the company. "We got ahead of our capacity to execute," said Henry Schacht, who came back from retirement to replace McGinn after he was fired in October 2000. The collapse of the telecommunications bubble eventually took down almost every player, but Lucent's decline began even before that. The company fell sooner, harder, and farther than its competitors.

In a technological marketplace moving at Internet speed, McGinn did not change the slow-moving and bureaucratic Western Electric culture. Lucent's structure was cumbersome, and its financial control system was woefully inadequate. For example, executives couldn't get information about profit by customer, product line, or channel, so they had no way of making good decisions about where to allocate resources. McGinn's people asked him in vain to fix this situation. He failed to confront nonperforming executives or replace them with people able to act as decisively as their counterparts at competitors such as Cisco and Nortel.

As a result, Lucent consistently fell short of technical milestones for new product development, and it missed the best emerging market opportunities. The company spent an enormous amount to install SAP, enterprise software that connects all parts of the company through a standard software platform, but the money was largely wasted because the company didn't change work processes to take advantage of it.

Lucent did meet its financial targets during the first two years, surfing on its customers' unprecedented wave of capital investment. But these early revenue gains came largely from Lucent's old voice-network switch business—a business with unsustainable growth prospects. Even before the wave broke, the company was struggling to deliver on McGinn's commitments.

A leader with a more comprehensive understanding of the organization would not have set such unrealistic goals. The hottest demand was for products Lucent didn't have, including the routers that guide Internet traffic and optical equipment with high capacity and bandwidth. Bell Labs was working on both of these products, but was painfully slow to develop and introduce them.

The missed opportunities in routers and optical gear are widely perceived as strategic errors. In fact, they show how execution and strategy are intertwined. In 1998 Lucent talked with Juniper Networks about acquiring it but then decided to develop routers in-house. But one part of execution is knowing your own capability. Lucent didn't have the capability to get its products to market fast enough. At the very least, good execution would have kept growth projections from getting so far out of hand when the company didn't have a presence in one of the hottest growth markets.

Similarly, the strategic error in optical gear originated with poor execution—in this case, the failure to understand changes in the external environment. As early as 1997, Lucent engineers were pleading with senior management to let them develop fiber optic products. But the leadership was used to listening its biggest customers—AT&T, its former parent, and the Baby Bells—and those customers had no interest in optical gear. This is a classic case of the so-called innovator's dilemma—companies with the greatest strength in a mature technology tend to be least successful in mastering new ones. But the innovator's dilemma itself has an execution solution that isn't generally recognized. If you're really executing, and you have the resources, you are listening to tomorrow's customers as well as today's and planning for their needs. Nortel was hearing the same arguments from its big customers, but it saw the emerging needs and organized itself to supply them.

Second, in the mad rush to grow revenues, Lucent set out in too many directions at once. It added myriad unprofitable product lines and acquired businesses it couldn't integrate—or even run, especially in the many cases where leaders of the acquired companies left because they couldn't abide the bureaucratic culture. Costs ran wild. The three dozen acquisitions, along with a roughly 50 percent increase in the workforce to some 160,000, led to redundancies, excess costs, and lowered visibility.

The endgame began well before the telecommunications market imploded. Under pressure to meet unrealistic growth projections, people left to their own devices did anything they could. Salespeople extended extraordinary amounts of financing, credit, and discounts to customers. They promised to take equipment that customers couldn't later sell. Some recorded products as being sold as soon as they were shipped to distributors. The result was a ravaged balance sheet. In 1999, for example, while revenues grew 20 percent, accounts receivable rose twice as fast, to over $10 billion. The company also amassed a huge amount of debt, largely from financing its acquisition binge, that put it near bankruptcy. It forced Lucent to sell businesses at fire-sale prices. The situation became so serious that the company flirted with losing its independence through its relationship with the French company Alcatel.

During the tech boom, neither industry people nor investors imagined that business could possibly drop so sharply. A leader skilled in execution would have probed his organization to get a realistic assessment of its market risks. According to published accounts, McGinn did not do so. And during his last year in office, he clearly was completely out of touch. Several times he had to revise financial estimates downward. To the very weekend when the board fired him, he insisted Lucent was dealing with its problems.

In a postmortem, the *Wall Street Journal* reported:

> *People familiar with the company say several executives told Mr. McGinn as long as a year ago that the company needed to drastically cut its financial projections because its newest products weren't ready yet and sales of older ones were going to decline.*
>
> *"He absolutely rejected" the advice, says one person familiar with the discussion. "He said the market is growing and there's absolutely no reason why we can't grow. He was in total denial."*
>
> *Indeed, in a recent interview, Mr. McGinn said that during Lucent's spectacular rise to stardom in the years after its spinoff from AT&T, he never gave much thought to how or whether the company might fall from grace.*

45

EXECUTING AT EDS

Now let's look at a formerly troubled company whose new CEO brought the discipline of execution. EDS had a lot in common with Xerox when Dick Brown took the helm in January 1999. EDS created its field, computer services outsourcing, and had been successful for decades. Then the information technology market changed, and EDS didn't. Competitors like IBM grabbed the growth. Revenues were flat, earnings declining, and the stock price sinking.

Like Thoman, Brown came from another industry—in his case, telecommunications. He'd previously turned around Cable & Wireless, the British telecommunications giant. At EDS, he faced a deeply embedded culture in need of fundamental change, one that was indecisive and lacking accountability, along with an organizational structure that no longer fit the needs of the marketplace. Two more parallels: not long after arriving, Brown set goals for revenue and earnings growth so ambitious that most people in the company thought them impossible to meet. And he subjected the company to a massive reorganization.

There the similarities end. Brown is deeply execution-oriented, and there was never any doubt who was in charge. While he points out that the transformation of EDS is still a work in progress, he successfully changed the fundamentals of the company in two years. He infused it with an energy and focus it hadn't experienced since its early days, and he met his profit and growth goals.

Brown's vision was that EDS could grow strongly and profitably by meeting the fast-growing new needs for information technology services. These services range from digitization within companies to virtual retailing and electronic integration, where companies work with suppliers, clients, and other service providers as if they were one integrated business. Keeping abreast of the changes was a big challenge for even the best corporate IT department and a serious problem for companies with limited resources.

Brown saw that EDS had the core competencies to serve these markets. These resources ranged from expertise in providing the most routine operational services at low cost to strategic consulting at the highest levels through its consulting firm, A.T. Kearney, acquired in 1995. Its people's breadth and depth of technical expertise and experience in solving clients' problems was a vast reserve of intellectual capital. One good thing about the EDS culture was a powerful can-do spirit. What one executive called "a belief we could do things for clients that seemed impossible" was the legacy of founder Ross Perot.

But EDS was trapped in its old structure and culture. Its forty-odd strategic business units (SBUs) were organized along industry lines, such as communications, consumer goods, and state health care. They divided the company into a confederation of fiefdoms, each with its own leaders, agenda, staffs, and sometimes policies. These fiefdoms rarely worked together, and the new marketplace opportunities were falling between the stools. How would Brown apply the company's intellectual capital to the new environment? EDS would need a new organizational structure, but first Brown had to change the culture to one of accountability and collaboration.

Brown jumped out onto the playing field. First, he got to know the company intimately, traveling around the globe for three months, meeting people at all levels formally and informally to talk and listen. In weekly e-mails that he sent to the whole organization, he not only told employees what he was thinking but also asked them to respond and make suggestions.

His candid and down-to-earth messages weren't simply communications—they were a tool for changing attitudes. They made the company's goals, issues, and new leadership style clear to the employees everywhere. And they put pressure from below on managers to explain priorities and open up their own dialogues.

Brown increased the quality and flow of information in other ways, too. For example, sales figures, which had formerly been compiled quarterly, were now reported daily, and for the first time the top 150 or so senior leaders were given the company's vital information, from profit margins to earnings per share.

Starting at the highest levels, Brown created new ways to drive accountability and collaboration. In the monthly "performance call," for example, he, his COO, and his CFO began hosting Monday-morning conference calls of the company's roughly top 150 leaders. These calls are essentially an ongoing operating review, in which the company's performance for the previous month and the year to date is compared with the commitments people have made. The calls provide early warning of problems and instill a sense of urgency. People who fall short have to explain why, and what they are going to do about it.

In the early days, when Brown was building the new culture of execution, the calls also served to reinforce the new standards of accountability. "The point I tried to make is that when you sign up for what used to be a budget item, you are committing for your team and each other," he says. "The rest are depending on you. It added a layer of weight and responsibility that was missing before."

The calls have brought a new reality to discussions of EDS operations. The talk is straightforward, even blunt, designed to elicit truth and coach people in the behavior

Brown expects of his managers. "Intense candor," Brown calls it, "a balance of optimism and motivation with realism. We bring out the positive and the negative." The calls can be uncomfortable for those in the negative column. In front of their peers, executives have to explain why and what they're doing to get back on track. "If your results are negative enough," adds Brown, "we'll talk after class." Such talks involve a series of questions and suggestions about what actions the executive plans to take to get back to performing on plan.

But neither the calls nor the "after class" discussions are scold sessions. As one senior executive (who has been with EDS since the beginning) says, "It's done in a positive and constructive way, not to embarrass. But just by the fact that it happens, human nature says you want to be one of the ones doing well."

The talk isn't always about numbers. At one of the first meetings, Brown recalls, "one of the executives made the statement that he was worried about growing anxiety and unrest in his organization, worried about rapid and dramatic change. His people were asking, 'Are we moving too fast, are we on the threshold of being reckless? Maybe we should slow down, take it easy, reflect a bit.'"

Brown turned the issue around—not incidentally, creating a forceful coaching lesson. "I jumped all over that. 'This is a test of leadership,' I said. 'I would like anybody on this call who is really worried about where we are going and worried about the fact that we will probably fail, tell me so right now. Don't be afraid to say you are. If you think we're making a big mistake and heading for the reef, speak up now.'

"No one did. So I said, 'If you're not worried, where's the worry coming from? I'm not worried, and you're not worried. Here's where it is: some of you say one thing, and your body language says another. You show me an organization that's wringing its hands, listening to rumors, anxious about the future, and I will show you leadership that behaves the same way. People imitate their leaders. If your organization is worried, you've got a problem, because you said you're not.'

"And I put it right back on that. 'Here's your test of leadership; now calm your organization, give them information; strike right at the heart of their worries. I can't believe that their worry is fact-based. I believe their worry is ignorance-based. And if that's the case, it's your fault.' "

Brown organized a series of two-day meetings for the top 150 executives, exposing them for the first time to the to the details of the company's plans, critical issues, and finances. "I want you to see the business from my level," he told them at the first one. "It engages you in what we're doing. It will focus you on the most critical issues we face." The meetings also gave diverse people practice in working together, not only at the meetings but throughout the year. "Know each other so when we collaborate and work together, we've got a face with a memo or an e-mail or a name," he said. "We're on the same team, and we can only get there working together."

People selection got intense attention. Brown removed scores of underperforming executives. Under new leadership, the HR department (renamed Leadership and Change Management) developed a compensation system that linked rewards to performance, along with a Web-based set of evaluation tools to help line executives sharpen their assessments of their people. Also added were extensive training courses for leaders at all levels, targeted to specific organizational needs. Leaders who couldn't handle all the changes either got coaching or were removed.

Brown himself ordered an analysis of the sales staff's performance and found, among other things, that 20 percent of the salespeople had sold nothing at all for the previous six months. He said to his sales executives, "What are you going to do about these people—and about their supervisors?" The 20 percent were replaced.

In its total impact on the company, Brown's reorganization was far bigger and more complex than the one that brought Xerox to its knees. Brown essentially turned EDS upside down. The SBUs were rolled into a new organization of four lines of business (LOBs) centered on broad market segments. E Solutions would offer a complete range of services for the "extended enterprise," linked electronically with suppliers and clients, from supply chain networks to Internet security. Business Process Management would provide businesses and governments with administrative and financial processing and client relationship management. Information solutions would sell IT and communications outsourcing, managed storage, and management of desktop systems. And A.T. Kearney would specialize in high-end consulting, along with executive search services. (EDS has since added a fifth LOB, PLM Solutions, which offers digitized product life cycle management—from development to collaboration with suppliers—for manufacturing companies.)

The new structure was more than a way to divide up business according to markets. It was designed so that EDS could fully leverage its intellectual capital for the first time, drawing on people from all parts of the company to provide solutions for clients. Collaboration among the lines of business would enable EDS to bring every client a value proposition based on its full "end-to-end" capability—from business strategy consulting to process redesign and management to Web hosting. It wouldn't work unless the people from the old business units learned not only their new jobs but also new ways of working together. At the same time, they were under orders to raise productivity at a 4 to 6 percent annual rate, making about $1 billion a year available for reinvestment or the bottom line. Moreover, the speed of new product introduction and delivery could not slacken.

The radical overhaul succeeded because Brown put its design in the hands of the people who would have to make it work. A team of seven executives was assembled from different disciplines and regions to come up with the new model. Meeting regularly with Brown, his COO, and the CFO, they produced the model in ten weeks of seven-day-a-week effort.

Simply in terms of the demands it made of EDS leaders, the new organization could not have been more different from the old one. In the past, the heads of business units were focused solely on the success of their part of the company. The new model, however, was designed to maximize results for the company as a whole, requiring close collaboration among all of the businesses. For most of the executives, the experience was their first taste of such teamwork. It wasn't always easy. Here's what one member had to say about the process:

> "We were seven people from different backgrounds with different views and different opinions. Some were more sales-oriented, some more delivery-oriented, some internationally focused, some very industry-knowledgeable. And we had to agree up

*front that the model we produced was one that we
all completely bought into.*

*"Getting there was really hard. I can tell you we
had lots of fights among ourselves. We stormed out
of the building and didn't like each other some
days. Compromise is difficult for me. I'm a very
strong, opinionated person. There were lots of
times when I was really frustrated. And there were
days when I would leave our meetings, and I'd get
in my car, and I would literally think, 'We're
destroying this company.' I've got twenty years in
the company; it's family to me, and I love it here. I
couldn't stand to think that we were destroying it.*

*"It takes some, I guess, emotional and mental
processing to make such a radical change, to understand that 'Hey, what we did before doesn't always
have to be the way we do it in the future, and you
just have to be open to it.' And at the end we
became personally close because we had to wrestle
through all the points together. So it truly, truly was
a good developmental experience."*

While all this was going on, Brown sharpened the company's focus on the quality of service it delivered to its
clients, which had slipped over the years. "Service excellence" became not only a mantra, but also an objective figuring in the performance rewards of all client-facing
executives and LOB presidents. Today 91 percent of EDS
clients rate their service either "good" or "excellent."

The results are evident in EDS's performance. At the end
of 2001, the company had achieved record revenues and
solid market share gains, and chalked up eleven consecutive quarters of double-digit growth in operating margins

and earnings per share. Its stock price was up some 65 percent from the time Brown took the job. After the executive session of the December 2001 board meeting, each EDS director approached Brown, and one by one told him they hadn't expected him to succeed in transforming the culture in less than three years, while at the same time delivering the stellar top- and bottom-line performance he'd achieved.

■ ■ ■

Each of the previous three companies we've talked about was once an icon of American business. Xerox, Lucent (as Western Electric and Bell Labs), and EDS created their industries, led them for years, and once were the companies against which competitors benchmarked themselves. Today two are struggling to recapture a small fraction of their former glory, while the third has regained its luster and aims to lead its industry once again. The difference? Execution.

The discipline of execution is based on a set of building blocks that every leader must use to design, install, and operate effectively the three core processes rigorously and consistently. Chapters 3 to 5 distill our observations about these building blocks: the essential behaviors of the leader, an operational definition of the framework for cultural change, and getting the right people in the right jobs.

PART II
THE BUILDING BLOCKS
OF EXECUTION

Building Block One: The Leader's Seven Essential Behaviors

What exactly does a leader who's in charge of execution do? How does he keep from being a micromanager, caught up in the details of running the business? There are seven essential behaviors that form the first building block of execution:

- *Know your people and your business.*
- *Insist on realism.*
- *Set clear goals and priorities.*
- *Follow through.*
- *Reward the doers.*
- *Expand people's capabilities.*
- *Know yourself.*

KNOW YOUR PEOPLE AND YOUR BUSINESS

Leaders have to *live* their businesses. In companies that don't execute, the leaders are usually out of touch with the day-to-day realities. They're getting lots of information delivered to them, but it's filtered—presented by direct reports with their own perceptions, limitations, and agendas, or gathered by staff people with their own perspectives. The leaders aren't where the action is. They aren't engaged with the business, so they don't know their organizations comprehensively, and their people don't really know them.

LARRY: Suppose a leader goes to a plant or business headquarters and speaks to the people there. He is sociable and courteous. He shows superficial interest in his subordinates' kids—how well they're doing in school, how they like the community, and so on. Or he chats about the World Series, the Super Bowl, or the local basketball team. He may ask some shallow questions about the business, such as "What's your level of revenue?" This leader is not engaged in his business.

When the visit is over, some of the managers may feel a sense of relief, because everything seemed to go so well and pleasantly. But the managers who are any good will be disappointed. They'll ask themselves, *What was the point?* They had prepared for tough questions—good people like to be quizzed, because they know more about the business than the leader. They'll feel frustrated and drained of energy. They didn't get a chance to make a good impression on the leader—and the leader certainly didn't make a good impression on them.

And of course, the leader hasn't learned anything. The next time he makes prognostications about the company, the press or the securities analysts may be awed, but the people in the business will know better. They'll ask each other, "How on earth could he say those things so confidently when he doesn't have a clue about what's happening down here?" It's kind of like the American politicians who used to visit Vietnam, look around a bit, talk to the top brass in the military command, review some statistics, and then proclaim that the war was being won and they could see the light at the end of the tunnel. Right!

When I go to a plant, it's because I've heard some things about the manager, and I need to confirm what I've heard about her. If I've heard she's effective, I'm going to try to reinforce her abilities. I'll have an in-depth discussion. I know she's going to do some good things, but I may leave her with a couple of thoughts she didn't have. If I've heard she's ineffective, I'll be making a decision about whether she can do the job or not. And I want to see what kind of a team she has, so I may just poke around at questions to get a clearer and more informed impression.

Next I meet with as many people in the plant as I can. I spend half an hour taking them through a slide presentation about where the company is. Then I take questions for an hour. I can sense from the questions and the dialogue how well the manager normally communicates with her workforce. If nobody asks me questions, I know this is not an open community. If people are afraid to ask me a tough question like "What's your bonus going to be this year?" I know this isn't going to be a free exchange.

The union leader's there too. He hears my story and asks if there will be any more layoffs. My answer is, "We haven't decided that. Customers help decide whether or not a plant stays open. In this case we had to become cost competitive—and fast. That means plant productivity has to dramatically improve." The point is that when you probe, you learn things and your people learn things. Everybody gains from the dialogue. And you dignify the leadership at the plant level by allowing them to expound on the business.

Here's a typical example of such a trip. A few months after I returned to Honeywell, I went to a plant in Freeport, Illinois, that makes sensors. It was an old Honeywell business, not on the cutting edge of contemporary practices, except that it had a very productive Six Sigma effort and a very productive digitization effort. Nobody had asked the leadership to institute these things. They just decided they were the right things to do. The manager who ran the plant was very smart.

"Your organization looks fine," I told him, but there were problems too. We talked in depth about his staff. "How long have these people been here or in the same job?" I asked. Too many of them had been there too long. "These are good people," I said, "but let's move them, promote them, so you can bring in some others once in a while to get some new insights. You've got to bring in some other people once in a while to get fresh thoughts, or you're always basically washing yourself in the same dishwasher. In other words, you've listened to all of the ideas of the people in the place, and you miss out on the fresh perspective of newcomers."

Then I asked why his quality staff reported to manufacturing. "That's like putting the fox in charge of guarding the chicken coop," I said. "I want quality to be analyzing manufacturing." Then I asked, "Why isn't the business development man here? You want to do some acquisitions, and he's off doing something else today, but he really should be here talking with me." He gave me a lame answer. Then he took me through the products that the plant produces and did a nice job.

But he had missed his forecast. "We didn't see the downturn coming," he said. When I asked him why, he wasn't sure—he told me he used a system based on the industrial production index, which has a 74 percent correlation with his business. I probed and found out that it was 74 percent in hindsight—it's not predictive. We talked about it a bit, and he agreed he'd try to find something that would be more helpful. But less than the index itself, I was interested in the way he *thought* about how it predicted the revenues in his business.

Then I talked to his staff along with him. When I met with him again afterward, I said, "You've got nine plants for a $600 million business. You've got to have fewer." He knew that, but now he had to decide which ones to close. Also, the plants made everything needed to produce the products. "You've got to outsource some of this stuff to other companies who can do it more cost-effectively," I told him. "And by the way, decide what to outsource before you decide which plants to close, because we want to know what the final footprint will look like."

People in the meeting had told me they had made some technological breakthroughs. But they didn't have a patent attorney, so I asked who protected the intellectual property. I asked about e-auctions—and told the manager that he had to be buying some stuff that way these days; it was less expensive. He admitted they were behind the curve there. Finally, the company had a hodgepodge of systems (a common problem, by the way). I told him he had to make these systems talk to each other without spending a fortune. He told me he'd figure out how.

Here's the good news, though. I was trying to revive the company's Six Sigma program, which had been let go in my absence. But this manager's Six Sigma program was right on top of things. It needed a little work, but he had plenty of black belts—people with the highest expertise in the discipline. His people were working on the right projects, and they had all the right metrics for customers. His digitization effort was very nice too. And again, he did it all with no influence from headquarters. That was impressive.

Here's what we both came away with about how to make the business better. He had to get some mix in people so they didn't all go brain-dead talking to each other. He could not have so many plants. He had to do more outsourcing to get his costs competitive. He had to protect his intellectual property—that was our competitive advantage. He needed to start using e-auctions so he could purchase in a more intelligent way. And he had to figure out how best to integrate his systems.

I left him with a few critical challenges, but he was a very impressive guy in a bad year. He was doing the right things, and he knew what to do about what he hadn't done.

■ ■ ■

What did the visit accomplish?

RAM: First, both parties came away with a clear agreement about what the manager needed to do to make the business better. Second, it was a great coaching exercise. Larry's tough questions got the manager to see the realities of his business more clearly and connected them with the external environment. The manager and his people saw the CEO-level view of competitive advantage. And the dialogue schooled them in how to think about the business in a more rigorous and analytical way. Third, Larry encouraged and motivated the plant team, creating energy. This is the modus operandi of a consistent process that makes a company more competitive.

The key word is "consistent." Leaders who are connected have distilled the challenges facing the business

unit they are visiting into a half dozen or fewer fundamental issues. These challenges do not change much over
short periods of time, and the way leaders like Larry master the total company is through a short list that cut across
multiple business units.

Being present allows you, as a leader, to connect personally with your people, and personal connections help
you build your intuitive feel for the business as well as for
the people running the business. They also help to per-
sonalize the mission you're asking people to perform.
Dick Brown's personal connections at all levels of the
organization at EDS fostered a degree of commitment and
passion that simply wouldn't have existed otherwise. We
know of no great leaders, whether in business, politics,
the military, religion, or any other field, who didn't have
these personal connections.

LARRY: As a leader, you have to show up. You've got
to conduct business reviews. You can't be detached and
removed and absent. When you go to an operation and
you run a review of the business, the people may not like
what you tell them, but they will say, "At least he cares
enough about my business to come and review it with us
today. He stayed there for four hours. He quizzed the hell
out of us." Good people want that. It's a way of raising
their dignity. It's a way of expressing appreciation and a
reward for their extensive preparation.

It's also a way to foster honest dialogue, the kind that
can sometimes leave people feeling bruised if they take it
personally. But the dialogue should not be mean-spirited.
Let's assume you have a heated debate with somebody.
You disagree with what he's doing, but then you both
resolve it one way or another. You can write the man a
note and say, "Great discussion yesterday about the

growth plan for your group. Appreciate your setting forth your views and your candor and insistence that we confront reality." You're not going home mad, and you don't want him going home mad. You're trying to promote the ability to intellectually debate important points. It doesn't matter who wins or loses. The fact that the debate happened and a resolution occurred is good in itself.

At Honeywell, after I do a business review, I write the leader a formal letter summarizing the things he agreed to do. But then I also write a personal note to the leader and say, "Gary, nice job yesterday. Productivity is not up to standards, and you need to work on it. Otherwise things are going great." It's just a note, takes five minutes. But those cards are all over the company—people show them around, and they save them.

If a manager is having trouble, you don't want to threaten to fire him—you want to help him with his problem. The personal connection makes that easier too. So you keep working on the personal connection every way you can. And then when he calls you up one day and says, "I've got another offer to go to another company," you know him; he knows you. And you say, "Well, Sam, why do you want to do that? You're doing well here. You've got a good future," and so on. Most times you can keep them. Absent that personal connection, you're just a name.

Making a personal connection has nothing to do with style. You don't have to be charismatic or a salesperson. I don't care what your personality is. But you need to show up with an open mind and a positive demeanor. Be informal, and have a sense of humor. A business review should take the form of a Socratic dialogue, not an interrogation. All you've got to prove is that you care for the people who are working for you. Whatever your respective personalities are, that's the personal connection.

■ ■ ■

The personal connection is especially critical when a leader starts something new. The business world is full of failed initiatives. Good, important ideas get launched with much fanfare, but six months or a year later they're dead in the water and are abandoned as unworkable. Why? Down in the organization, the managers feel that the last thing they need is one more time-consuming project of uncertain merit and outcome, so they blow it off. "This too will pass," they say, "just like the last bright idea of the month." Result: the company wastes time, money, and energy, and the leader loses credibility, usually without realizing that the failure is a personal indictment.

The leader's personal involvement, understanding, and commitment are necessary to overcome this passive (or in many cases active) resistance. She has not only to announce the initiative, but to define it clearly and define its importance to the organization. She can't do this unless she understands how it will work and what it really means in terms of benefit. Then she has to follow through to make sure everyone takes it seriously. Again, she can't do this if she can't understand the problems that come with implementation, talk about them with the people doing the implementing, and make clear—again and again—that she expects them to execute it.

RAM: In the mid-1990s, a friend told Jack Welch about a new methodology for making a quantum increase in inventory turns in manufacturing operations. Relatively few business leaders back then understood what a powerful tool faster inventory turnover was for generating cash and increasing return on investment. GE, the friend said, could generate cash if it could increase its inventory turns across the company. He gave Welch the name of a leading practitioner of this methodology, Emmanuel Kampouris, the CEO of American Standard. At that time—in the mid 1990s—American Standard had achieved in some plants as high as forty inventory turns compared to the average of four at most companies.

Welch was excited by the idea, but he was not content to get just the concept—he wanted to understand the workings personally. Rather than sending some of his manufacturing people out to investigate it, he paid a visit to Kampouris and spent several hours with him.

Then he followed through to learn the hows at ground level. He accepted an invitation to speak at American Standard. During the dinner that followed, he sat between two of Kampouris's plant managers, one from Brazil and one from the U.K., whose plants had achieved annual inventory turns of 33 and 40, respectively. Welch spent the whole evening questioning them closely about the details—the tools, the social architecture, how they overcame resistance to the new methodology.

Didn't the chairman of GE have better things to do with his time? Absolutely not! By involving himself deeply and personally with the subject, Welch learned what it would take to execute such an initiative at GE. He learned what skills and attitudes would be required of people, and what resources would be needed. Thus he was able to get the necessary changes rolling quickly throughout his huge company. By the time Welch retired in 2001, inventory turns had doubled, to 8.5.

INSIST ON REALISM

Realism is the heart of execution, but many organizations are full of people who are trying to avoid or shade reality. Why? It makes life uncomfortable. People don't want to open Pandora's box. They want to hide mistakes, or buy time to figure out a solution rather than admit they don't have an answer at the moment. They want to avoid confrontations. Nobody wants to be the messenger who gets shot or the troublemaker who challenges the authority of her superiors.

Sometimes the leaders are simply in denial. When we ask leaders to describe their organization's strengths and weaknesses, they generally state the strengths fairly well, but they're not so good on identifying the weaknesses. And when we ask what they're going to *do* about the weaknesses, the answer is rarely clear or cohesive. They say, "We have to make our numbers." Well, of course you have to make your numbers; the question is *how* you are going to make your numbers.

Was it realistic for AT&T to acquire a bunch of cable businesses it didn't know how to run? The record shows it wasn't. Was it realistic for Richard Thoman to simultaneously launch two sweeping initiatives at Xerox without being able to install the critical leaders? Clearly not.

How do you make realism a priority? You start by being realistic yourself. Then you make sure realism is the goal of all dialogues in the organization.

LARRY: Embracing realism means always taking a realistic view of your company and comparing it with other companies. You're always keeping an eye on what's happening in companies around the world, and you're measuring your own progress, not internally, but externally. You don't just ask, "Have I made progress from last year to this year?" You ask, "How am I doing vis-à-vis other companies? Have they made a lot more progress?" That's the realistic way to look at your station.

It's shocking to see how many people don't want to confront issues realistically. They're not comfortable doing it. When I took over at AlliedSignal, for example, I got two different pictures from our people and our customers. While our people were saying that we were delivering an order-fill rate of 98 percent, our customers thought we were at 60 percent. The irony was, instead of trying to address the customer's complaints, we seemed to think we had to show that we were right and they were wrong.

At the roundtables I hold when I go out to visit facilities, I ask people, "What are we doing right in this business, and what are we doing wrong in this business?" Then I'll ask, "What do you like about Honeywell, and what don't you like?" Some people just have gripes, while others go after me personally. But most have good information and insights. I make notes and take them up afterward with the manager.

When I visit management classes at the training center, I talk for ten minutes, answer questions for a half an hour or so, and then go around shaking hands with everyone and asking them the same questions I ask at the roundtables. And so people leave with the understanding that realism matters. They go back and tell their bosses, "Well, you know, I saw Bossidy. I told him what was wrong." And their bosses will know that I know.

Learning takes place on both sides. I may learn, for example, that lack of collaboration between two businesses prevents generation of new revenue from customers. Or that an important initiative is not getting a high enough priority in some business units. On the other side they find out about the company as a whole—where I see real progress and where I'm dissatisfied.

SET CLEAR GOALS AND PRIORITIES

Leaders who execute focus on a very few clear priorities that everyone can grasp. Why just a few? First, anybody who thinks through the logic of a business will see that focusing on three or four priorities will produce the best results from the resources at hand. Second, people in contemporary organizations need a small number of clear priorities to execute well. In an old-fashioned hierarchical company, this wasn't so much of a problem—people generally knew what to do, because the orders came down through the chain of command. But when decision making is decentralized or highly fragmented, as in a matrix organization, people at many levels have to make endless trade-offs. There's competition for resources, and ambiguity over decision rights and working relationships. Without carefully thought-out and clear priorities, people can get bogged down in warfare over who gets what and why.

A leader who says "I've got ten priorities" doesn't know what he's talking about—he doesn't know himself what the most important things are. You've got to have these few, clearly realistic goals and priorities, which will influence the overall performance of the company.

For example, Lucent's main goal in 2002 is to survive until demand for its products comes back. Its debt is so high that its debt rating has been lowered, and it has come close to violating covenants with lenders. So Lucent's first priority is to conserve cash. This translates into keeping receivables and inventories to a minimum, selling assets that are not really needed, outsourcing manufacturing, and reducing costs. Its second priority is to focus on customers so it can build a durable revenue base. This priority is on the minds of everyone, and has a huge influence on day-to-day behavior.

Along with having clear goals, you should strive for simplicity in general. One thing you'll notice about leaders who execute is that they speak simply and directly. They talk plainly and forthrightly about what's on their minds. They know how to simplify things so that others can understand them, evaluate them, and act on them, so that what they say becomes common sense.

Sometimes it takes a new pair of eyes to clarify priorities. In August 2000, the world's largest retail chain in its category named a new CEO. The chain was losing ground to competitors. Caught up in the excitement of "revolutionary" ambitions, it had pursued e-commerce and other new non-store ventures, and had lost its focus on executing the core business. Its stock price had fallen by two-thirds over the past year.

The senior management team urged the new CEO to grow the business by building more stores. But the CEO, who had risen through the company as a block-and-tackle execution-oriented person, felt the company was already chasing too many possibilities. He made improving the performance of existing stores his top priority, and focused his people on raising gross margins and comparable sales (improving same-store sales from year to year).

He took three steps to translate these goals into actions. First he sat down with his ten direct reports to explain the goals and discuss their implementation—how they could be met, what obstacles had to be overcome, and how the incentive system had to be changed. Then he gathered his roughly top 100 merchandising and store executives for a two-day session. He taught them about the anatomy of the business, explaining directly and simply such things as what had happened to sales growth and why; what factors, such as logistics flow, were affecting the cost structure; and how harmony between the merchandising people and the stores was missing and what the consequences were. He set clear targets for the next four quarters and discussed with them how to meet the targets. Before the executives left, each had a ninety-day action plan and clear agreement on following through. Finally, he conducted a similar two-day session for several hundred merchandising and store managers.

As of December 2001, the chain's gross margins had improved dramatically, and its stock price had doubled.

FOLLOW THROUGH

Clear, simple goals don't mean much if nobody takes them seriously. The failure to follow through is widespread in business, and a major cause of poor execution. How many meetings have you attended where people left without firm conclusions about who would do what and when? Everybody may have agreed the idea was good, but since nobody was named accountable for results, it doesn't get done. Other things come up that seem more important, or people decide it wasn't such a good idea after all. (Maybe they even felt that way during the meeting, but didn't speak up.)

For example, a high-tech company was hit hard by the recession of 2001, suffering a 20 percent decline in revenue. The CEO was reviewing the revised operating plan for one of his most important divisions. He congratulated the division president on how well he and his people had reduced its cost structure, but noted that the business would still fall short of its target for return on investment. And he offered a possible solution. He'd recently learned about the importance of velocity, and suggested that the division could make real gains by working with its suppliers to increase inventory turnover. "What do you think you can do?" he asked the purchasing manager. The manager replied that with some engineering help, he thought he could make substantial improvements. "I'd need twenty engineers," the manager added.

The CEO turned to the engineering vice president and asked him if he would assign the engineers to the task. The vice president hemmed and hawed for half a minute. Then he said, in chilly tones, "Engineers don't want to work for purchasing." The CEO looked at the vice president for several moments. Finally he said: "I am *sure* you will transfer twenty engineers to purchasing on Monday." Then he walked toward the door, turned, and looked at the purchasing executive, and said: "I want you to set up a monthly videoconference with yourself, engineering, the CFO, and me and the manufacturing manager to review the progress of this important effort."

What did the CEO do here? First he surfaced a conflict that stood in the way of achieving results. Second, by creating a follow-through mechanism, he ensured that everyone would indeed do what they were supposed to. This included the division president, who had sat passively on the sidelines until the CEO delivered his ultimatum. And the CEO's action sent a signal through the rest of the company that others, too, could expect follow-through actions.

REWARD THE DOERS

If you want people to produce specific results, you reward them accordingly. This fact seems so obvious that it shouldn't need saying. Yet many corporations do such a poor job of linking rewards to performance that there's little correlation at all. They don't distinguish between those who achieve results and those who don't, either in base pay or in bonuses and stock options.

LARRY: When I see companies that don't execute, the chances are that they don't measure, don't reward, and don't promote people who know how to get things done. Salary increases in terms of percentage are too close between the top performers and those who are not. There's not enough differentiation in bonus, or in stock options, or in stock grants. Leaders need the confidence to explain to a direct report why he got a lower than expected reward.

A good leader ensures that the organization makes these distinctions and that they become a way of life, down throughout the organization. Otherwise people think they're involved in socialism. That isn't what you want when you strive for a culture of execution. You have to make it clear to everybody that rewards and respect are based on performance.

In chapter 4, we'll explain why so many companies don't reward the doers, and how those that execute do.

EXPAND PEOPLE'S CAPABILITIES THROUGH COACHING

As a leader, you've acquired a lot of knowledge and experience—even wisdom—along the way. One of the most important parts of your job is passing it on to the next generation of leaders. This is how you expand the capabilities of everyone else in your organization, individually and collectively. It's how you will get results today and leave a legacy that you can take pride in when you move on.

Coaching is the single most important part of expanding others' capabilities. You've surely heard the saying, "Give a man a fish, and you'll feed him for a day; teach a man how to fish, and you'll feed him for a lifetime." That's coaching. It's the difference between giving orders and teaching people how to get things done. Good leaders regard every encounter as an opportunity to coach.

RAM: The most effective way to coach is to observe a person in action and then provide specific useful feedback. The feedback should point out examples of behavior and performance that are good or that need to be changed.

When the leader discusses business and organizational issues in a group setting, everybody learns. Wrestling with challenging issues collectively, exploring pros and cons and alternatives, and deciding which ones make sense increases people's capabilities both individually and collectively—if it's done with honesty and trust.

The skill of the coach is the art of questioning. Asking incisive questions forces people to think, to discover, to search. Here's an example I observed in a planning review

74

at a major American multinational company. The head of one of the largest business units was explaining his strategy for taking his division from third place in its European market to first. An ambitious plan, it depended on making sharp and swift market share gains in Germany. "That was an inspiring presentation," said the CEO after it was over. But, he noted, Germany was the home base of the unit's most powerful global competitor, which was four times its size. "How are you going to make those gains?" he asked. "What customers are you going to acquire? What products and what kind of competitive advantages will you need to beat the German competitor and gain and sustain market share?"

The division head didn't have answers to these business questions. The CEO then turned to evaluating organizational capability. "How many salespeople do you have?" he asked. "Ten," the leader answered. "How many does your main competitor have?" The answer—I could barely hear the man, he was so sheepish—"Two hundred." The CEO's last question was more of a statement. "Who runs Germany for you? Wasn't he in another division until a few months ago? How many levels are there between you and the person running Germany?"

With a few simple but critical questions, the CEO had exposed weaknesses in the strategy that would have made it a certain failure in execution.

Many CEOs would have ended the dialogue there, leaving the business leader chastened and miserable. And in doing so they would have missed an important opportunity to coach all the leaders at the meeting, helping them with both their personal growth and the company's growth. But this CEO's aim was to educate his team on planning realistically.

"There may be a way to make this plan work," he observed. "Instead of trying a broad assault, why not segment the market and look for the competitor's weak spots, winning on speed of execution? Where are the gaps in his product line? Can you innovate something that will fill them? Can you identify and focus on the customers who are most likely to buy such products?"

At the meeting's end, the leader—energized by the challenge—agreed to rethink the plan and return in ninety days with a more realistic alternative. And everybody learned an important lesson about the anatomy of the strategy process.

■ ■ ■

The same principles apply to coaching an individual privately. Whatever your style—whether it's gentle or blunt—your aim is to ask the questions that bring out the realities and give people the help they need to correct problems.

LARRY: Let's say you've got a person making all the numbers, making all his commitments, but his behavior is terrible. Charlie's working people seven days a week, he hollers, and he won't hire a woman. You call him in and say, "I love you, Charlie, but the things you're doing are going to preclude you from making numbers down the road. People aren't going to put up with this nonsense anymore. You've got a couple of choices. I'm going to be your coach. I'm going to talk to you myself. And I want this behavior changed, or you're not going to go any farther, or you're going to have to leave."

Charlie may argue that his behavior's not so bad. You give him the evidence: "Okay, I've got ten people here

76

who say it *is* bad. Are they all wrong? You don't keep them in here on weekends? I've got a logbook with dates that says all your people are in here Saturdays and Sundays. I've told everybody around here, 'I don't want you in here every Sunday.' Is that a lie?" "No." "Well, then your behavior is bad, right?" "Right." "Now, let's think about how we're going to fix it. This isn't a disaster, but you've got to fix it."

Sometimes people like Charlie do fix it and sometimes they don't. If they don't, you've got to get rid of them, because ultimately it will affect results. So it isn't just numbers; it's behavior.

Education is an important part of expanding people's capabilities—if it's handled right. Many companies are almost promiscuous about it, offering cornucopias of generic courses in management or leadership and putting far too many people into them.

In one company I know every bonus-eligible manager went through the executive development program. It was an absolute waste of time for 50 percent of them. You need to make judgments about which people have the potential to get something useful out of a course and what specific things you're trying to use education to accomplish, in order to expand the capabilities of the organization.

At Honeywell our learning strategy is based on the kind of organizational capabilities people need. Some of these include tools people have to master—Six Sigma, digitization, managing the flow of materials through a work cell by self-directed teams. Some are broader, having to do with executive development. Here the best learning comes from working on real business problems. We ask people look to at three or four issues facing the company, and we form them into teams to work on those issues.

Keep in mind that 80 percent of learning takes place outside the classroom. Every leader and supervisor needs to be a teacher; classroom learning should be about giving them the tools they need.

KNOW YOURSELF

Everyone pays lip service to the idea that leading an organization requires strength of character. In execution it's absolutely critical. Without what we call emotional fortitude, you can't be honest with yourself, deal honestly with business and organizational realities, or give people forthright assessments. You can't tolerate the diversity of viewpoints, mental architectures, and personal backgrounds that organizations need in their members in order to avoid becoming ingrown. If you can't do these things, you can't execute.

It takes emotional fortitude to be open to whatever information you need, whether it's what you like to hear or not. Emotional fortitude gives you the courage to accept points of view that are the opposite of yours and deal with conflict, and the confidence to encourage and accept challenges in group settings. It enables you to accept and deal with your own weaknesses, be firm with people who aren't performing, and to handle the ambiguity inherent in a fast-moving, complex organization.

RAM: You surely have noticed that the best leader is often not the most brilliant person in the outfit, or the one who knows most about the business. What gives this person more confidence to be a leader than others who are demonstrably better in one dimension or another?

Here's a clue. A certain executive lacked an essential

quality that he needed to be a strong leader. He was the CEO of a large company I worked with, who had two executive vice presidents reporting to him. One VP, responsible for about 60 percent of the company's business, was an old and trusted colleague, completely loyal to the CEO. But he was faltering. In his gut, the CEO knew it, but he was unable to make the tough decision to let him go. (It wasn't the first time the CEO had faced this issue and frozen; that other time somebody else cleaned up the mess.) Eventually the board ordered the CEO to get rid of him. With that, the power passed to the board, and the inevitable consequence was that the CEO himself went shortly thereafter.

This man was smart and pleasant to people, and he knew the business. But he didn't have emotional fortitude. On the contrary, he had an emotional blockage that kept him from dealing forthrightly with the inadequacy of his executive vice president. Psychologists know that some people are limited, even crippled, by emotional blockages that prevent them from doing things that leadership requires. Such blockages may lead them to avoid unpleasant situations by ducking conflicts, procrastinating on decisions, or delegating with no follow-through. On the darker side, they may drive the leader to humiliate others, draining energy and sowing distrust.

■ ■ ■

Emotional fortitude comes from self-discovery and self-mastery. It is the foundation of people skills. Good leaders learn their specific personal strengths and weaknesses, especially in dealing with other people, then build on the strengths and correct the weaknesses. They earn their leadership when the followers see their inner strength, inner confidence, and ability to help team members deliver results, while at the same time expanding their own capabilities.

A solid, long-term leader has an ethical frame of reference that gives her the power and energy to carry out even the most difficult assignment. She never wavers from what she thinks is right. This characteristic is beyond honesty or beyond integrity, beyond treating people with dignity. It's a business leadership ethic.

Leaders in contemporary organizations may be able to get away with emotional weakness for a brief time, but they can't hide it for long. They face challenges to their emotional strength all the time. Failure to meet these challenges gets in the way of achieving results. Getting things done depends ultimately on performing a specific set of behaviors. Without emotional fortitude, it's tough to develop these behaviors, either in ourselves or in others. How can your organization face reality if people don't speak honestly, and if its leaders don't have the confidence to surface and resolve conflicts or give and take honest criticism? How can a group correct mistakes or get better if its members don't have the emotional fortitude to admit they don't have all the answers?

Putting the right people in the right jobs requires emotional fortitude. Failure to deal with underperformers is an extremely common problem in corporations, and it's usually the result of the leader's emotional blockages. Moreover, without emotional fortitude, you will have a hard time hiring the best people to work for you. Because if you are lucky, these people will be better than you are; they will bring new ideas and energy to your operation. A manager who is emotionally weak will avoid such people out of fear that they will undercut his power. His tendency will be to protect his fragile authority. He will surround himself with people he can count on to be loyal and exclude those who will challenge him with new thinking. Eventually, such emotional weakness will destroy both the leader and the organization.

In our years of working and observing in organizations, we have pinpointed four core qualities that make up emotional fortitude:

AUTHENTICITY: A psychological term, *authenticity* means pretty much what you might guess: you're real, not a fake. Your outer person is the same as your inner person, not a mask you put on. Who you are is the same as what you do and say. Only authenticity builds trust, because sooner or later people spot the fakers.

Whatever leadership ethics you may preach, people will watch what you do. If you're cutting corners, the best will lose faith in you. The worst will follow in your footsteps. The rest will do what they must to survive in a muddy ethical environment. This becomes a pervasive barrier to getting things done.

SELF-AWARENESS: Know thyself—it's advice as old as the hills, and it's the core of authenticity. When you know yourself, you are comfortable with your strengths and not crippled by your shortcomings. You know your behavioral blind sides and emotional blockages, and you have a modus operandi for dealing with them—you draw on the people around you. Self-awareness gives you the capacity to learn from your mistakes as well as your successes. It enables you to keep growing.

Nowhere is self-awareness more important than in an execution culture, which taps every part of the brain and emotional makeup. Few leaders have the intellectual firepower to be good judges of people, good strategists, and good operating leaders, and at the same time talk to customers and do all the other things the job demands. But if you know where you're short, at least you can reinforce those areas and get some help for your business or unit. You put mechanisms in place to help you get it done. The person who doesn't even recognize where she is lacking never gets it done.

SELF-MASTERY: When you know yourself, you can master yourself. You can keep your ego in check, take responsibility for your behavior, adapt to change, embrace new ideas, and adhere to your standards of integrity and honesty under all conditions.

Self-mastery is the key to true self-confidence. We're talking about the kind that's authentic and positive, as opposed to the kinds that mask weakness or insecurity—the studied demeanor of confidence, or outright arrogance.

Self-confident people contribute the most to dialogues. Their inner security gives them a methodology for dealing with the unknown and for linking it to the actions that need to be taken. They know they don't know everything; they are actively curious, and encourage debate to bring up opposite views and set up the social ambience of learning from others. They can take risks, and relish hiring people who are smarter than themselves. So when they encounter a problem, they don't have to whine, cast blame, or feel like victims. They know they'll be able to fix it.

HUMILITY: The more you can contain your ego, the more realistic you are about your problems. You learn how to listen and admit that you don't know all the answers. You exhibit the attitude that you can learn from anyone at any time. Your pride doesn't get in the way of gathering the information you need to achieve the best results. It doesn't keep you from sharing the credit that needs to be shared. Humility allows you to acknowledge your mistakes. Making mistakes is inevitable, but good leaders both admit and learn from them and over time create a decision-making process based on experience.

LARRY: No one does the leader's job flawlessly, believe me. You've got to make mistakes and learn from them. Yankees manager Joe Torre got fired three times during his career. Now he's looked upon as the icon of the game. He learned some things along the way.

In his book, *Jack: Straight from the Gut,* Jack Welch freely admits he made many hiring mistakes in his early years. He made a lot of decisions from instinct. But when he was wrong, he'd say, "It's my fault." He'd ask himself why he was wrong, he'd listen to other people, he'd get more data, and he'd figure it out. And he just kept getting better and better. He also recognized that it's not useful to beat other people up when they make mistakes. To the contrary, that's the time to coach them, encourage them, and help them regain their self-confidence.

■ ■ ■

How do you develop these qualities in yourself? There are, of course, books on the subject, some of them useful. Many companies, including GE and Citicorp, include self-assessment tools in their leadership development programs.

But the ultimate learning comes from paying attention to experience. As people reflect on their experiences, or as they get coached, blockages crumble and emotional strengths develop. Sometimes the ahas also come from watching others' behavior: your observational capabilities make you realize that you too have a blockage that you need to correct. Either way, as you gain experience in self-assessment, your insights get converted into improvements that expand your personal capacity.

Such learning is not an intellectual exercise. It requires tenacity, persistence, and daily engagement. It requires reflection and modifying personal behavior. But my experience is that once an individual gets on this track, his or her capacity for growth is almost unlimited.

The behavior of a business's leaders is, ultimately, the behavior of the organization. As such, it's the foundation of the culture. In the next chapter, we present a new framework for changing the culture of an organization.

CHAPTER 4

Building Block Two:
Creating the Framework
for Cultural Change

When a business isn't going well, its leaders often think about how to change the corporate culture. They're right to recognize that the "soft" stuff—people's beliefs and behaviors—is at least as important as hard stuff, such as organizational structure, if not more so. Making changes in strategy or structure by itself takes a company only so far. The hardware of a computer is useless without the right software. Similarly, in an organization the hardware (strategy and structure) is inert without the software (beliefs and behaviors).

Most efforts at cultural change fail because they are not linked to improving the business's outcomes. The ideas and tools of cultural change are fuzzy and disconnected from strategic and operational realities. To change a business's culture, you need a set of processes—social operating mechanisms—that will change the beliefs and behavior of people in ways that are directly linked to bottom-line results.

In this chapter, we present a new reality-based framework for cultural change that creates and reinforces a discipline of execution. This approach is practical and completely linked to measurable business results.

The basic premise is simple: cultural change gets real when your aim is execution. You don't need a lot of complex theory or employee surveys to use this framework. You need to change people's behavior so that they produce results. First you tell people clearly what results you're looking for. Then you discuss how to get those results, as a key element of the coaching process. Then you reward people for producing the results. If they come up short, you provide additional coaching, withdraw rewards, give them other jobs, or let them go. When you do these things, you create a culture of getting things done.

RAM: I was observing a meeting at a newly formed division of a company in the Fortune 20. The division, with some 20,000 employees, was the product of a merger in 2001 of two companies in the same industry. It had a new leadership team, and this was only its second meeting. The central issue for the leadership team was how to create a new culture to improve unacceptable performance. Return on capital was less than 6 percent, and shareholder value was being destroyed. The new CEO of the division and the leadership team knew that cost savings through synergies would not be enough to make the division an outstanding performer.

The general practice in both merged businesses was not to hold people accountable for commitments they had made individually. Under the rubric of so-called teamwork, each management team performed poorly. For example, each had lost market share and suffered from lower return on investment because its people did not reduce costs in logistics ahead of competitors. This task is one that is truly under management's control, but the leader in charge of logistics received the same reward as other members of the management team.

The team had hired a human behavior boutique consulting firm that specialized in cultural diagnostics. The consultant had performed a standard cultural analysis based on surveys that asked employees fifty or sixty questions about the division's values (integrity, honesty, and the like), whether decision making was autocratic or collegial, and how power was distributed. The results were stylishly presented, but nothing in the survey showed *how* the division could work differently in terms of its beliefs and behaviors so that it would achieve outstanding business results.

The discussion at the meeting was going nowhere until, in her characteristic probing style, the division's CEO took over and started by asking the right question. "If we want to change the culture, what should be our next question?"

One member of the team asked in response, *"How should the culture be changed?"* A second member said, "Make it better." Then someone asked: *"From what to what?"* and the lightbulb went on.

The CEO divided the team into groups of six and asked each to find ten pairs of "from what to what." The groups wrote down some big words: "from nonperformance culture to performance culture"; "from static to continuous improvement"; "from domestic to globally oriented." But specificity was missing.

The CEO bore in and challenged the groups to make the list more specific and to find one "from what to what" change that, if carried out, would dramatically improve

87

the behavior of the key people who drove the behavior of everyone else in the division. Since most people have difficulty in being this specific, the CEO took the next step: she divided the leadership team into two-person teams and asked each pair to identify one idea about what the culture was now and what should it become.

The teams agreed that improving accountability would be the most important change. Then the leader asked, "Where does that begin?" and the answer was: "With this team." Then the leader asked, "Are you willing to hold each of us accountable?" There was a stunned silence. "But if you don't practice the right behavior in this team, will anyone else in the organization?" he asked. No answer was needed.

The final question was: "After we change our group's behavior, what do we do next?" The head of HR said, "Communicate it to twenty thousand people." The leader asked, "How would that make anyone change? It won't work by itself. What *will* work is the practice of accountability beginning right here with this team. After we hold ourselves accountable, the next phase is for this team to hold the three hundred managers in this division accountable for their performance, without which three thousand supervisors and seventeen thousand employees will not experience the culture and discipline of execution." Then they discussed specific action steps for putting accountability into the culture at the top of the division and the three hundred managers reporting to the top team. They would have follow-through, feedback, and rewards tied to individual performance and behavior. The behavior included each management team member holding each of their direct reports accountable as well.

■ ■ ■

OPERATIONALIZING CULTURE

There's a saying we recently heard: We don't think ourselves into a new way of acting, we act ourselves into a
new way of thinking.

Acting your way into a new way of thinking begins
with demystifying the word *culture*. Stripped to its essentials, an organization's culture is the sum of its shared values, beliefs, and norms of behavior. People who are setting
out to change a culture often talk first about changing the
set of values. That's the wrong focus. Values—fundamental principles and standards, such as integrity or respect
for the customer or in GE's case boundarylessness—may
need to be reinforced, but they rarely need changing.
When people, especially those at the highest levels of the
company, violate one of the company's basic values, the
leader must step forth to publicly condemn those viola-
tions. Anything less is interpreted as a lack of emotional
fortitude.

The beliefs that influence specific behaviors are more
likely to need changing. These beliefs are conditioned by
training, experience, what people hear inside or outside
about the company's prospects, and perceptions about
what leaders are doing and saying. People change them
only when new evidence shows them persuasively that
they're false. For example, if people in an organization
believe they're in a mature industry with no growth
prospects, they won't spend a lot of time and energy inten-
sively looking for growth opportunities. If they believe
others who do less than they do will get the same rewards,
that belief will drain their energy.

One of Dick Brown's first priorities at EDS was to

change the culture by focusing on beliefs and behaviors. At a meeting of the EDS senior leadership team in January 2000, he asked people to identify the most critical beliefs that had shaped the company's view of itself in the past five years and the beliefs most needed now for the journey forward. Working in groups, they came up with the following lists.

Old EDS Beliefs

- *We are in a commodity business.* EDS is in a slow-growth, mature industry—computer services outsourcing—that has lots of competition, little differentiation, and thus inherently low profit margins.

- *We can't grow at market rates.* As the biggest player in a commodity business, EDS has difficulty finding profitable growth.

- *Profits follow revenues.* If EDS can get more business, it will somehow make money on it. (This belief is a formula for misallocating resources.)

- *Each leader owns all resources—control is key.* Each division has total autonomy and safeguards its turf. (This belief makes collaboration among business units impossible.)

- *My peer is my competitor.* (Like owning the resources, this belief is a major barrier to success. Internally competitive behavior is destructive. The competitor is out there in the marketplace, not in the next unit. Teamwork, sharing of knowledge, and cooperation are absolutely essential to winning in the market.)

- *People aren't accountable ("it's not my fault").*

- *We know more than our clients.*

- *Our people will tell the client what solutions he or she needs.* (This belief prevented EDS people from adequately listening to their clients' problems and needs.)

New EDS Beliefs

- *We can grow faster than the market—profitably, and using capital efficiently.*
- *We can increase productivity year in and year out.*
- *We are committed to our clients' success.*
- *We will achieve service excellence.*
- *Collaboration is the key to our success.*
- *We are going to be accountable and committed.*
- *We will be better listeners to our clients.*

The second list became an agenda for attitude change, not only among the top executives but for all of EDS's leaders.

Behaviors are beliefs turned into action. Behaviors deliver the results. They're where the rubber meets the road. When we talk about behavior, we are talking less about individual behavior than about norms of behavior: the accepted, expected ways groups of people behave in the corporate setting—the "rules of engagement," as some people call them. The norms are about how people work together. As such, they are critical to a company's ability to create a competitive advantage.

LINKING REWARDS TO PERFORMANCE

The foundation of changing behavior is linking rewards to performance and making the linkages transparent. A business's culture defines what gets appreciated and respected and, ultimately, rewarded. It tells the people in the organization what's valued and recognized, and in the interest of trying to make their own careers more success-ful, that's where they will concentrate. If a company rewards and promotes people for execution, its culture will change.

Far too many companies do a poor job of linking rewards to performance. What's the problem?

RAM: While some leaders in some companies success-fully make this link, too many behave like wimps. We've seen again and again that people love to give rewards; they love to be loved. But they don't have the emotional fortitude to give honest feedback and either withhold a reward or penalize people. They don't feel comfortable rewarding performance and behavior. They procrastinate, sugarcoat, and rationalize. Leaders sometimes even create new jobs for nonperformers. As a result, the organization below is totally confused.

At EDS, Dick Brown moved quickly to make sure the performers got rewarded more than the nonperformers. Lack of accountability had been a major problem in the company, as the leadership ranks well understood. "There were no negative consequences for poor performance," recalled one executive. "Not only no consequences, but if you were part of the good old boy network, there really wasn't accountability for negative behavior toward the company." Added another, "It was always somebody else's problem."

Brown instituted a system that ranked all executives in quintiles by how well they performed compared with their peers, and rewarded them accordingly. It is similar to the "vitality curve" Jack Welch introduced at GE to differentiate "A," "B," and "C" players.

Ranking people in this fashion generates controversy when managers design and execute the system clumsily—using it, for example, to arbitrarily force a certain percentage of people out of the organization. But if coupled with coaching that gives subpar performers the opportunity to improve themselves, it can greatly help introduce a results-oriented culture. The process has to have integrity: the right information must be collected and used, based on behavior and performance criteria. Leaders must give honest feedback to their people, especially those who end up in the bottom rankings.

That's what Brown did. For example, he says, "In the first year, a person came to me and said, 'Your system doesn't work. Last year I was rated really well. This year I did the same work and achieved the same level of performance, but I was rated really low.' I said, 'Well, let me give you an answer. It's one of two things or both. Number one, chances are you weren't as good as you thought you were last year. Number two, if you *were* that good and you did the same job this year, you're rated lower because you didn't get any better, and everyone else did. You've got to realize, EDS is improving, and everybody's got to improve the job they do, and if you're staying the same, you're falling behind.'"

EDS also factors individuals' behavior into its rewards. Collaboration, for example, was important to the success of the new business model, but in the old EDS there was very little collaborative behavior. So in the incentive portion of their compensation, leaders are now evaluated and rewarded in part on how well they work together. Suppose Bob, in one line of the business, develops a client, then gives the client to Linda in another line, because her unit can better serve the client. His sacrifice will be noted in his evaluation, and his organization leader will take it into account in setting his bonus. Salespeople get specific incentives for business they deliver to other lines of business.

Whatever approach you use to determine rewards, the goal is the same: the compensation system has to have the right yields. You should reward not just strong achievements on numbers but also the desirable behaviors that people actually adopt. You should increase the population of A-players, defined as those who are tops in both behavior and performance. You should remove the nonperformers. Over time, your people will get stronger and you'll get better financial results.

LARRY: You get what you measure for, and it's a straightforward process. At the beginning of the year, I write a letter to each of Honeywell's business leaders and staff leaders and say, "This is what we agreed are your goals." The first component is the financial goals—revenue growth, income, cash flow, productivity, or other variables depending on the nature of the business and what we're trying to accomplish at that particular time. The goals will be weighted according to the nature of the business. For example, if a business needs to develop four new products, I may lower the goal for sales growth and productivity and raise the goal for product introductions.

The second component would be other goals, focused on what we're doing both this year and in the long term.

These goals could be anything from creating the Six Sigma infrastructure to breaking into a specific marketplace. We formally evaluate performance and potential twice a year in our management resource reviews. And then we link the results of the evaluations to compensation.

The general manager of each business gives specific goals to each of his direct reports. They may all have the same financial goals, but they'll have different nonfinancial ones—building a stronger organization, working on diversity, or whatever the key issue of the day is.

You want differentiation among options, among bonuses, and among salary increases. Differentiation is the mother's milk of building a performance culture. For the top 250 people, I use stock options. We stay competitive on base salaries, but anybody who wants to make a lot of money at Honeywell has got to make it on options. Here again, they're not an entitlement. For example, I've got a seasoned professional who's good at his job but doesn't exhibit further potential. I'm going to pay him a tidy cash bonus but give him a lower allocation of stock options and maybe none in stock grants. On the other hand, someone else seems to have a lot of potential, but if she didn't do as good a job in one year as I would have liked, I'm going to give her less cash, but I'm going to continue to motivate her with options because I think she's an asset to the company's future.

We do all we can to reward people for doing their best. That's how we got a performance culture. Here's one example: in 2002 many companies will be handing out small bonuses or none at all, given the state of the economy. Our aerospace component was hit harder than most by the terrorist attacks of September 11, and very few of its businesses will match the previous year's results. But we're measuring the people on how well they perform against their competitors in this kind of environment. If they do better, they will receive bonuses.

■ ■ ■

Linking rewards to performance is necessary to creating an execution culture, but it's not enough by itself. All too commonly a tough new leader, striving for a performance culture, will set rigorous performance standards and then stand back to watch the play unfold. "Sink or swim" is the message. Lots of people proceed to sink, and the organization may sink too, as Sunbeam did with Al Dunlap.

Other leaders design rewards for new behaviors of execution but implement them brutally. They don't take the important step of helping people to master the new required behaviors. They don't coach. They don't teach people to break a major concept down into smaller critical tasks that can be executed in the short term, which is difficult for some people. They don't conduct the dialogues that surface realities, teach people how to think, or bring issues to closure.

■ ■ ■

The missing part of the equation lies in what we call the social software of execution.

THE SOCIAL SOFTWARE OF EXECUTION

RAM: How many meetings have you attended where everyone seemed to agree at the end about what actions would be taken but nothing much actually happened as a result? These are the meetings where there's no robust debate and therefore nobody states their misgivings. Instead, they simply let the project they didn't like die a quiet death over time.

In my career as an adviser to large organizations and their leaders, I have witnessed many occasions even at the highest levels when silent lies and a lack of closure lead to false decisions. They are "false" because they eventually get undone by unspoken factors and inaction. These instances of indecision share a family resemblance—a misfire in the personal interactions that are supposed to produce results. The people charged with reaching a decision and acting on it fail to connect and engage with one another. Intimidated by the group dynamics of hierarchy and constrained by formality and lack of trust, they speak their lines woodenly and without conviction. Lacking emotional commitment, the people who must carry out the plan don't act decisively.

These faulty interactions rarely occur in isolation. Far more often, they're typical of the way large and small decisions are made—or not made—throughout a company. The inability to act decisively—which translates into an inability to execute—is rooted in the corporate culture and seems to employees to be impervious to change.

The key word here is "seems," because, in fact, leaders create a culture of indecisiveness, and leaders can break it. The primary instrument at their disposal is the social software of the organization.

Like a computer, a corporation has both hardware and software. We call the software of the corporation "social software" because any organization of two or more human beings is a social system.

The hardware includes such things as organizational structure, design of rewards, compensation and sanctions, design of financial reports and their flow. Communication systems are part of the hardware. So is a hierarchical distribution of power, where such things as assignment of tasks and budget-level approvals are visible, hardwired, and formal. The social software includes the values, beliefs, and norms of behavior, along with everything else that isn't hardware. Like the computer's software, it's what brings the corporate hardware to life as a functioning system.

Structure divides an organization into units designed to perform certain jobs. The design of structure is obviously important, but it is the software that integrates the organization into a unified, synchronized whole. Hardware and software in combination create the social relationships, the norms of behavior, the power relationships, flows of information, and flows of decisions.

For example, basic reward systems are hardware because they're quantitative. You make your numbers, the system rewards you according to a formula, and congratulations, here's the check. But if you want to reward other behaviors—your record with Six Sigma or in improving the diversity of your leadership team or your collaboration with peers—software enters the picture, because it defines the norms of behavior being rewarded. Leaders who create disproportionate awards for high performers and high-potential people are creating social software that drives behaviors: people work harder at differentiating themselves.

■ ■ ■

A key component of software is what we call Social Operating Mechanisms. These are formal or informal meetings, presentations, even memos or e-mail exchanges—anywhere that dialogue takes place. Two things make them operating mechanisms, not just meetings. First, they're integrative, cutting across the organization and breaking barriers among units, functions, disciplines, work processes, and hierarchies and between the organization and the external environment as well. Social Operating Mechanisms create new information flows and new working relationships. They let people who normally don't have much contact with one another exchange views, share information and ideas, and learn to understand their company as a whole. They achieve transparency and simultaneous action.

Second, Social Operating Mechanisms are where the beliefs and behaviors of the social software are practiced consistently and relentlessly. They spread the leaders' beliefs, behaviors, and mode of dialogue throughout the organization. Other leaders learn to bring these beliefs and behaviors to the lower-level formal and informal meetings and interactions they conduct, including coaching and feedback. They become *their* Social Operating Mechanisms. And so on down the line.

Linked to one another and to the measurement and reward systems, the Social Operating Mechanisms collectively become what we call the Social Operating System of the corporation. As such, they drive its culture. In the people, strategy, and operations processes, for example, the review sessions that draw the company's top leaders together are the main Social Operating Mechanisms; the processes combined make up the Social Operating System.

GE's highly developed Social Operating System is central to the company's success. Its main Social Operating Mechanisms include the Corporate Executive Council (CEC), which meets quarterly; Session C, the annual leadership and organizational reviews; S-1 and S-2, the strategy and operating reviews; and Boca, an annual meeting in Boca Raton, Florida, where operating managers meet to plan the coming year's initiatives and re-launch current initiatives.

At CEC meetings, which run two and a half days, GE's roughly thirty-five top leaders review all aspects of their businesses and the external environment, identify the company's greatest opportunities and problems, and share best practices. The CEO also uses the forum to observe how his leaders think and how they work together, and to coach them.

A Session C meeting is an intense eight-to-ten-hour gathering where the CEO and head of HR meet with the business leaders and top HR executives of each business unit. They review the unit's prospective talent pool and its organizational priorities. Does GE have the right people in the right jobs to execute its strategies? Who needs to be promoted or rewarded, who needs help with development, who can't handle the job? The CEO follows up each session with a handwritten note reviewing the substance of the dialogue and the action items. Through this mechanism, picking and evaluating people has become a core competence at GE.

The S-1 strategy meeting takes place toward the end of the second quarter. Here the CEO, CFO, and members of the office of the CEO meet with each unit head and his or her team to discuss the strategy for the next three years, including the initiatives agreed upon by the CEC and the fit between the strategy and the people in charge of executing it. As with the Session C meetings, the CEO follows up with a letter to each leader outlining the action items they've agreed upon. The S-2 meeting, held in November, is the operating plan meeting that focuses more on the coming twelve to fifteen months, linking strategy to operational priorities and resource allocation.

In between, other Social Operating Mechanisms are at work. In April GE surveys some 11,000 employees online for feedback on how well the initiatives are taking hold throughout the organization. In October the 150 top corporate officers meet at the Crotonville Learning Center to review the progress of the initiatives, get operating plans rolling for the coming year, and participate in executive development courses. And at the December CEC meeting, among other things, executives set the agenda for January's Boca meeting.

This system of linked Social Operating Mechanisms is how GE's leaders unite a company of businesses so diverse that people have sometimes called it a conglomerate. The Social Operating System explicitly ties GE's overall strategy to the performance of each unit, including its leadership development and operating plans. The dialogue, a norm of behavior created by former CEO Jack Welch, is honest and reality-based. Feedback is candid. And the CEO is present and actively participating throughout, at every meeting. It's an operating system for execution.

The contemporary corporation is complex, and each of its many parts is constantly in motion: moving structures, moving ideas, moving decisions, and moving people all responding to a moving business environment. The Social Operating System is the constant. More than anything else, it provides the consistent framework that's needed to create common ways of thinking, behaving, and doing. Over time it transcends even deeply rooted local cultures.

LARRY: Our Social Operating System at Honeywell isn't as elaborate as GE's, but it serves the same purposes. All of our behaviors are evident in the people process, the strategy process, and the operations process and at two management meetings where more than a hundred of our leaders are in attendance. These meetings are where people practice those behaviors most intensely. From there it cascades down into the organization.

One of the most important things people take with them from the processes is the understanding of how to work together in constructive debate. No one person has all the ideas or all the answers. If we have a problem in one place, people will respond by getting together and finding a solution, not by sitting around and moaning that they don't have a solution or deciding to engage a consultant. We don't expect people to know everything, but we do expect people to get the best answers they can get, and they get them by working with other people. Practicing such constructive debates over time builds confidence in people to tackle unfamiliar issues as they arise.

THE IMPORTANCE OF ROBUST DIALOGUE

You cannot have an execution culture without robust dialogue—one that brings reality to the surface through openness, candor, and informality. Robust dialogue makes an organization effective in gathering information, understanding the information, and reshaping it to produce decisions. It fosters creativity—most innovations and inventions are incubated through robust dialogue. Ultimately, it creates more competitive advantage and shareholder value.

Robust dialogue starts when people go in with open minds. They're not trapped by preconceptions or armed with a private agenda. They want to hear new information and choose the best alternatives, so they listen to all sides of the debate and make their own contributions.

When people speak candidly, they express their real opinions, not those that will please the power players or maintain harmony. Indeed, harmony—sought by many leaders who wish to offend no one—can be the enemy of truth. It can squelch critical thinking and drive decision making underground. When harmony prevails, here's how things often get settled: after the key players leave the session, they quietly veto decisions they didn't like but didn't debate on the spot. A good motto to observe is "Truth over harmony." Candor helps wipe out the silent lies and pocket vetoes, and it prevents the stalled initiatives and rework that drain energy.

Informality is critical to candor. It was one of Jack Welch's bywords. Formality suppresses dialogue; informality encourages it. Formal conversations and presentations leave little room for debate. They suggest that everything is scripted and predetermined. Informal dialogue is open. It invites questions, encouraging spontaneity and critical thinking. At a meeting in a formal, hierarchical setting, a powerful player can get away with killing a good idea. But informality encourages people to test their thinking, to experiment, and to cross-check. It enables them to take risks among colleagues, bosses, and subordinates. Informality gets the truth out. It surfaces out-of-the-box ideas—the ideas that may seem absurd at first hearing but that create breakthroughs.

Finally, robust dialogue ends with closure. At the end of the meeting, people agree about what each person has to do and when. They've committed to it in an open forum; they are accountable for the outcomes.

The reason most companies don't face reality very well is that their dialogues are ineffective. And it shows in their results. Think about the meetings you've attended—those that were a hopeless waste of time and those that produced energy and great results. What was the difference? It was not the agenda, not whether the meeting started on time or how disciplined it was, and certainly not the formal presentations. No, the difference was in the quality of the dialogue.

In the typical corporate meeting—a business review, for example—the dialogue is constrained and politicized. Some people want to shade and soften what they say to avoid a confrontation. Others need to beat those they're talking to into submission. In groups that contain both types of people (which is the case in many meetings), dialogue becomes a combat sport for the killers and a humiliation or bore for the passives. Little reality gets on the table, and the meeting doesn't move the issues forward much.

Now think of a meeting that produced great results— that got to the realities and ended with a plan for results. How did it happen?

Dialogue alters the psychology of a group. It can either expand a group's capacity or shrink it. It can be energizing or energy-draining. It can create self-confidence and optimism, or it can produce pessimism. It can create unity, or it can create bitter factions.

Robust dialogue brings out reality, even when that reality makes people uncomfortable, because it has purpose and meaning. It is open, tough, focused, and informal. The aim is to invite multiple viewpoints, see the pros and cons of each one, and try honestly and candidly to construct new viewpoints. This is the dynamic that stimulates new questions, new ideas, and new insights rather than wasting energy on defending the old order.

How do you get people to practice robust dialogue

when they're used to the games and evasions of classical corporate dialogue? It starts at the top, with the dialogues of the organization's leader. If he or she is practicing robust dialogue, others will take the cue. Some leaders may be short on the emotional fortitude required to invite disagreement without getting defensive. Others may need to learn some specific skills to help people challenge and debate constructively. These people should be able to get help.

But the key is that people act their way to thinking because they're driven for results. If you reward for performance, the interest in performance will be sufficiently deep to sponsor a dialogue. Everybody needs to get the best answer, and that means everybody must be candid in their exchanges—no one person has all the ideas. If someone says something you disagree with and you rudely tell him he's full of hot air, a lot of other people aren't going to speak out next time. If instead you say, "Okay, let's talk about that. Let's listen to everybody and then make our choice," you'll get much better responses.

LEADERS GET THE BEHAVIOR THEY EXHIBIT AND TOLERATE

Once you understand social software, it becomes plain that no leader who's disengaged from the daily life of the business can possibly change or sustain its culture. As Dick Brown puts it, "The culture of a company is the behavior of its leaders. Leaders get the behavior they exhibit and tolerate. You change the culture of a company by changing the behavior of its leaders. You measure the change in culture by measuring the change in the personal behavior of its leaders and the performance of the business."

To build an execution organization, the leader has to be present to create and reinforce the social software with the desired behaviors and the robust dialogue. She has to practice them and drill them relentlessly in the social operating mechanisms.

For example, some leaders use regular conference calls as an operating mechanism to drive change in the culture by forcing new candor and realism into the dialogues and decision making of the company's top leaders. The calls introduce accountability and follow-through. The leader's own behavior, including her communications with people at all levels, modeled and reinforced the beliefs and behavior her people needed to learn.

The dialogue the leader conducts in these calls develops the total company picture for all to see. Everyone has come prepared to explain what will be done in the coming month to deliver on commitments if results are lagging expectations. By discussing the entire business and having a focus on the external environment, everyone participating knows more about overall trends, competition, issues, and roadblocks. If they are doing their job to help build a culture of execution, this information will cascade through the company.

■ ■ ■

Can you create an execution culture in your own business if it's part of a larger organization that doesn't have one? If you try, will you become a social outcast? The odds are that you can do it—especially once you start showing profit and revenue growth.

LARRY: You as a leader don't want to send your people out on hara-kiri missions, but I do think you can do it even if it's not part of a major corporate thrust. I always ran my reviews with the idea that you want to get the truth out. When I became a GE traveling auditor in the late 1960s, I visited GE locations all over the world, and I noticed a lot of different styles of managers. Watching the successful ones and the unsuccessful ones confirmed my feeling that the more you get involved and the better you hash the issues out on the table, the better the decisions you will make in terms of their resolution. These lessons stayed with me for the rest of my career.

When I became a GE Capital unit manager in 1978, I was following these practices. But in that year Jack Welch came in as consumer sector executive, and he intensified this process dramatically. It was more penetrating and it was more action-oriented, more what-are-you-going-to-do-about-it-oriented. He took what I had known and elevated it in terms of intensity. He gave the people process a depth and ardor and intensity that I hadn't seen before.

The more experience I got as a leader, the more I brought that experience to the processes. In the people process, for example, when I started, my first thought was always to see how good a person was in a job. After all, that's what made the business run. As time went on, I still talked about that, but I also kept thinking, *What is the growth potential of this person?* I began to ask a lot more questions and get dialogue going on long-range potential.

I also got more people involved in the discussion, because when you expand the audience, you know more. We used to have too many one-on-ones, because we didn't want something that was said candidly about a person to get out and be harmful. But we found a way to solve that problem. We acknowledged that the person being discussed was going to hear everything that was said in that room anyway, and we'd agree that we would be candid but professional. The conversations were still forthright, but they weren't damaging. We took care not to say anything about the person that you wouldn't say to his or her face.

I was born hands-on and have always been excited about my business. I'm enthusiastic, intrigued, and curious about it. And that's what determines whether you can make these changes in your organization. If you find them troublesome, if you find them trying, they won't work. You've got to like the process, otherwise it won't work.

■ ■ ■

Success in executing a cultural change depends first and foremost on having the right people. In the next chapter we turn to the most important job leaders do: selecting and evaluating people.

CHAPTER 5

Building Block Three: The Job No Leader Should Delegate—Having the Right People in the Right Place

Given the many things that businesses can't control, from the uncertain state of the economy to the unpredictable actions of competitors, you'd think companies would pay careful attention to the one thing they can control—the quality of their people, especially those in the leadership pool. An organization's human beings are its most reliable resource for generating excellent results year after year. Their judgments, experiences, and capabilities make the difference between success and failure.

Yet the same leaders who exclaim that "people are our most important asset" usually do not think very hard about choosing the right people for the right jobs. They and their organizations don't have precise ideas about what the jobs require—not only today, but tomorrow— and what kind of people they need to fill those jobs. As a result, their companies don't hire, promote, and develop the best candidates for their leadership needs.

Quite often, we notice, these leaders don't pay enough attention to people because they're too busy thinking about how to make their companies bigger or more global than those of their competitors. What they're overlooking is that the quality of their people is the best competitive differentiator. The results probably won't show up as quickly as, say, a big acquisition. But over time, choosing the right people is what creates that elusive sustainable competitive advantage.

Dell ultimately out-competed Compaq, a far bigger company, because Michael Dell took great pains to have the right people in the right jobs—people who understood how to execute his business model superbly. Nokia, a minor player in the cell phone industry early in the 1990s, became the global leader because of its people. Under the leadership of CEO Jorma Ollila, who had come from a bank to lead the struggling diversified company, they adopted digital technology sooner than Motorola, then the dominant company. They also saw that the cell phone was not a communications device but also a fashion item, and built excitement in the marketplace for their products with monthly introductions of new products.

If you look at any business that's consistently successful, you'll find that its leaders focus intensely and relentlessly on people selection. Whether you're the head of a multibillion-dollar corporation or in charge of your first profit center, you cannot delegate the process for selecting and developing leaders. It's a job you have to love doing.

LARRY: The most troubling problem I found when I joined AlliedSignal was the weakness of our operating management team—it wasn't up to par with our competitors. And we were unlikely to produce future leaders, because we didn't have any bench strength. When I retired from Allied Signal in 1999, I considered the greatest sign of our strength to be the extraordinary quality of our leadership pipeline. One measure of their quality was that several of our outstanding people had been recruited to lead other organizations, among them Paul Norris (who became CEO of W. R. Grace); Dan Burnham, hired as Raytheon's CEO; Gregory L. Summe (CEO of PerkinElmer); and Frederic M. Poses (CEO of American Standard).

That level of excellence didn't happen by accident. I had devoted what some people considered an inordinate amount of time and emotional energy to hiring, providing the right experiences for, and developing leaders—between 30 and 40 percent of my day for the first two years and a good 20 percent later. That's a huge amount of time for a CEO to devote to any single task, but I'm convinced it accounts in large part for AlliedSignal's success.

One of the first things I did was to visit the company's plants, meet the managers, and get a feel for their individual capabilities. I didn't just talk to them; I talked to their people as well, to see how they perceived their work environment and how they behaved—both of which reflect the kind of job a leader does. It was during those visits that I came to see that the company's inattention to leadership development was a major problem.

While I was impressed with my half-dozen direct reports, I was less impressed with the heads of our operating units and the teams they had built. Some of the managers simply needed seasoning in a few more assignments in different businesses. Too often, though, they lacked a well-rounded business foundation, so they set priorities from a functional standpoint. They didn't demonstrate basic skills like understanding the competition or developing their people. I'm not saying they weren't smart or didn't work hard. They had good ideas and knew how to present them, but they had not been prepared to execute. So we tried to give them generous severance packages and help them land on their feet.

The next step was to vigorously recruit more able people—not only to run our businesses but also to ensure that we could develop talented leaders in the future. Executive development needs to be a core competency. At GE 85 percent of the executives are promoted from within—that's how good the company is at developing leaders. And it got so good because Jack Welch—and now his successor, Jeff Immelt—made leadership development a top priority and demanded that all of his executives do the same. At AlliedSignal, by contrast, we had to go outside for nearly all our early hires, mostly to companies that had people-development processes at the level of GE and Emerson Electric.

Eventually we were able to fill most jobs from within, which had always been my goal. But it didn't happen without a lot of my personal involvement in appraising and developing leaders.

I evaluated not only my direct reports but also the direct reports of direct reports, and I sometimes went even further down the organization. In my first three years at AlliedSignal, I personally interviewed many of the three hundred new MBAs we hired, whom we considered our future leaders.

I couldn't interview everybody, but I knew that the standard I set would be followed in the rest of the organization: you hire a talented person, and they will hire a talented person.

WHY THE RIGHT PEOPLE
AREN'T IN THE RIGHT JOBS

Common sense tells us the right people have to be in the right jobs. Yet so often they aren't. What accounts for the mismatches you see every day? The leaders may not know enough about the people they're appointing. They may pick people with whom they're comfortable, rather than others who have better skills for the job. They may not have the courage to discriminate between strong and weak performers and take the necessary actions. All of these reflect one absolutely fundamental shortcoming: The leaders aren't personally committed to the people process and deeply engaged in it.

Lack of Knowledge

Leaders often rely on staff appraisals that focus on the wrong criteria. Or they'll take a fuzzy and meaningless recommendation for someone a direct report likes. "Bob's a great leader," the candidate's advocate exclaims. "He's a great motivator, a great speaker. He gets along with people, and he's smart as hell." The leader doesn't ask about the specific qualities that make Bob right for the job. Often, in fact, he doesn't have a good grasp of the job requirements themselves. He hasn't defined the job in terms of its three or four nonnegotiable criteria—things the person *must* be able to do in order to succeed.

RAM: In November 2001 I was having lunch with the head of a consumer products company and his vice chairman. The company had been losing market share, and the discussion at the table identified the source of the problem: weak marketing leadership at the top. The company clearly needed to hire a chief marketing person— it would be a make-or-break job for 2002. The CEO had someone in mind. She had been recommended by Mark, the vice chairman, and the CEO sang her praises, saying, "She's great, fantastic." "In what ways?" I asked. When he answered in glittering generalities, I pressed and again asked *why* he thought she was so wonderful. Remarkably, he couldn't be specific, and his face turned crimson.

I asked the CEO and the vice chairman what the three nonnegotiable criteria for the job were. After some discussion, they named the following: be extremely good in selecting the right mix of promotion, advertising, and merchandising; have a proven sense of what advertising is effective and how best to place this advertising in TV, radio, and print; have the ability to execute the marketing program in the right timing and sequence so that it is coordinated with the launch of new products; and be able to select the right people to rebuild the marketing department.

After they articulated these criteria for the job, I asked whether the candidate met them. There was a long silence. Finally the leader answered honestly: "You know, now I realize that I don't really know her."

Neither the CEO, the vice chairman, nor anyone else in the organization had asked the right questions. To consistently improve its leadership gene pool, every business needs a discipline that is embedded in the people process, with candid dialogues about the matches between people and jobs, and follow-through that ensures people take the appropriate actions.

Lack of Courage

Most people know someone in their organization who doesn't perform well, yet manages to keep his job year after year. The usual reason, we find, is that the person's leader doesn't have the emotional fortitude to confront him and take decisive action. Such failures can do considerable damage to a business. If the nonperformer is high enough in the organization, he can destroy it.

RAM: Several years ago an industrial fine-components manufacturing company concluded that it didn't have enough bench strength in its succession plan, so it hired two CEO candidates from the outside. The company was number one in its field globally, with a long record of success. One candidate, Stan, was hired to lead its North American operations, the crown jewel of the business that produced 80 percent of the company's profits. He'd come from a global electronics company in the same general field, where he'd run a small business unit. He presented himself well, connected with people quickly, was hardworking, and made dazzling presentations.

But Stan didn't do so well as head of North American operations. He missed his first year's financial commitments. He lost market share, and the cost structure of his operation became uncompetitive. The industry was suffering at the time from excess capacity, but Stan did not close plants, cut costs, or focus on execution. The company's margins and cash flow declined, and its stock price dropped like a rock. But the CEO took no action, feeling that Stan was still new and needed time to get into the culture, and that his coaching would put him on the right track.

Then Stan missed the second year's targets. Cash flow declined again, and the stock price dropped further. The board became very concerned. After Stan made his next quarterly report to them, the board met in executive session with the CEO and essentially told him to fire the man. But the move came too late to save the company. By this time, the stock price had been cut in half. The company became an inviting product for investment bankers and a target for aggressive, acquisition-minded companies. Within six months, it was taken over.

The CEO was very bright, a man of high integrity, always willing to give people the benefit of the doubt. He genuinely liked Stan. But he lacked the courage to confront poor performers, or force plant closings and layoffs. He failed to make the leader of his most important operation face the reality of the industry's situation, and failed to hold him accountable for his poor performance.

The Psychological Comfort Factor

Many jobs are filled with the wrong people because the leaders who promote them are comfortable with them. It's natural for executives to develop a sense of loyalty to those they've worked with over time, particularly if they've come to trust their judgments. But it's a serious problem when the loyalty is based on the wrong factors. For example, the leader may be comfortable with a person because that person thinks like him and doesn't challenge him, or has developed the skill of insulating the boss from conflict. Or the leader may favor people who are part of the same social network, built up over years in the organization.

RAM: The newly appointed CEO—I'll call him Howard—of a $25 billion global company was aggressive, ambitious, and enjoyed great press. Expectations were so high that before he retired in a decade, Howard would take the company from number three to number one in its fiercely competitive ten-player industry.

Howard asked all but three of the eleven-person senior leadership team to retire early, and replaced them with people loyal to him. Everything went well for the first two years, thanks to the previous management's efforts. In the third year, the business began to fall apart. Success in this industry required frequent new product introductions, and Howard's team missed one deadline after another by six months or more. The company lost share in its highest-margin product lines to foreign competitors who brought their products out on time, and the delays had a huge impact on the brand images.

The delays also increased launch costs by 15 percent, a serious financial penalty because the business is highly capital intensive, with low margins. The company's cash position deteriorated rapidly, its debt rating was downgraded twice, and it cut its dividend. Two of Howard's hand-picked direct reports were responsible for the increased costs and missed deadlines. A captive of his psychological comfort and blind loyalty, Howard would not replace them. Before the year was over, the board removed him and his team.

The sharpest contrast I know of to this sort of behavior happened at GE, when Reginald Jones picked Jack Welch to succeed him as chairman and CEO. Jones, who was born in the U.K., was cerebral, well-spoken, and considered one of the great business statesmen of his day. Welch was irreverent, blunt, worked from the gut, and loved to debate. On the surface he was the opposite of

Jones. But Jones recognized that GE had to change, and that Welch—who was smart, tenacious, and dedicated to excellence, as was Jones—had the right kind of intelligence and personality for the job ahead. Welch's rowdy informality masked a well-studied and incisive mind and an unparalleled desire to win.

Bottom Line: Lack of Personal Commitment

When the right people are not in the right jobs, the problem is visible and transparent. Leaders know intuitively that they have a problem and will often readily acknowledge it. But an alarming number don't do anything to fix the problem. You can't will this process to happen by issuing directives to find the best talent possible. As noted earlier, leaders need to commit as much as 40 percent of their time and emotional energy, in one form or another, to selecting, appraising, and developing people. This immense personal commitment is time-consuming and fraught with emotional wear and tear in giving feedback, conducting dialogues, and exposing your judgment to others.

But the foundation of a great company is the way it develops people—providing the right experiences, such as learning in different jobs, learning from other people, giving candid feedback, and providing coaching, education, and training. If you spend the same amount of time and energy developing people as you do on budgeting, strategic planning, and financial monitoring, the payoff will come in sustainable competitive advantage.

WHAT KIND OF PEOPLE
ARE YOU LOOKING FOR?

As we've noted earlier, in most companies people regard a good leader as one with vision, strategy, and the ability to inspire others. They assume that if the leader can get the vision and strategy right, and get his message across, the organization's people will follow. So boards of directors, CEOs, and senior executives are too often seduced by the educational and intellectual qualities of the candidates they interview: Is he conceptual and visionary? Is she articulate, a change agent, and a good communicator, especially with external constituencies such as Wall Street?

They don't ask the most important question: How good is this person at getting things done? In our experience, there's very little correlation between those who talk a good game and those who get things done come hell or high water. Too often the second kind are given short shrift. But if you want to build a company that has excellent discipline of execution, you have to select the doer.

LARRY: The person who is a little less conceptual but is absolutely determined to succeed will usually find the right people and get them together to achieve objectives. I'm not knocking education or looking for dumb people. But if you have to choose between someone with a staggering IQ and an elite education who's gliding along, and someone with a lower IQ but who is absolutely determined to succeed, you'll always do better with the second person.

I didn't always understand that. I too was of the mind that the better the education and pedigree, the smarter the person. But that's not true. You're searching for people with an enormous drive for winning. These people get their satisfaction from getting things done. The more they succeed in getting things done, the more they increase their capacity.

You can easily spot the doers by observing their working habits. They're the ones who energize people, are decisive on tough issues, get things done through others, and follow through as second nature.

■ ■ ■

We see this problem particularly when highly intellectual staff people or consultants want to move into high-level line jobs. They frequently come from the best business schools, from consulting firms and from internal jobs in finance, accounting, and strategic planning. The trouble is, they have never been tested in mobilizing line people to execute. They haven't had the experience that develops business instinct.

For example, Joan was the finance director of a high-growth division of an industrial products company. She wanted to go from her staff job, in which she had no chance to become CEO, to a line position, which would make her a candidate for succession. She became leader of the largest product line in the division, with full responsibility for market share, profit and loss, and balance sheet items like receivables and inventory. It became clear within twelve months to both the company CEO and the head of the division that she lacked important people skills to revitalize and refocus her direct reports, including replacing some people in key positions. She also did not demonstrate the courage to hold prices when customers demanded huge discounts in a recessionary economy.

We're not saying that staff people can never move into line jobs. In GE, for example, Jack Welch recognized early in his tenure as CEO that he needed additional sources of leadership talent. GE recruited from the best business schools and the top consulting firms into its strategic planning and marketing consulting units. The rule was that people who were successful would move into line jobs at levels below the business unit manager. There they were tested and had the opportunity to demonstrate whether they had the necessary people skills to become head of a unit. Jeff Immelt, the current CEO of GE, was recruited through this channel. Other prominent leaders who have moved from consulting firms or staff jobs include Louis Gerstner, chairman and, until recently, CEO of IBM; Jim McNerny, CEO of 3M; and Art Collins, CEO of Medtronics. Each had a chance to demonstrate his managerial skills.

They Energize People

LARRY: Some leaders drain energy from people and others create it. Suppose you interview someone who has great potential—he's got an elite education, good work experience, and high marks for achievement. But he's docile and reserved—he just sits there. Sometimes people like that just don't interview well, and if he's had great success, I may have to take a lot more time looking at his record before approving or disapproving him. But I'm wary about hiring him for an important leadership job. He's likely to pick people like himself, and you'll have to ring a bell to wake them up. I want people who arrive in the morning with a smile on their faces, who are upbeat, ready to take on the tasks of the day or the month or the year. They're going to create energy, and energize the people they work with—and they're going to hire people like that too.

■ ■ ■

We're not talking about inspiring people through rhetoric. Too many leaders think they can create energy by giving pep talks, or painting an uplifting picture of where the business can be in a few years if everybody just does their best. The leaders whose visions come true build and sustain their people's momentum. They bring it down to earth, focusing on short-term accomplishments—the adrenaline-pumping goals that get scored on the way to winning the game.

Bob Nardelli, the current chairman and CEO of the Home Depot, is an example of such an energizer. In his previous job he headed GE Power Systems, which he transformed from a moribund business into one of the company's stellar divisions. He took over at Power Systems in 1995, after a successful stint at the Transportation Systems division (which Jack Welch had used as a place to test executives who seemed to have potential to rise higher). Earlier, Nardelli had also run one of GE's consumer businesses. Power Systems had half of the world market for large power generating equipment, but the business was in a major slump—utilities had cut back sharply on capital investment, and no rebound was in sight. Nardelli had a vision for growing by enlarging the business's pond—expanding its offerings to include smaller generating equipment, moving into new industry segments, and providing not only equipment but services to its customers. At first he ran into disbelief and resistance from a bureaucratic culture whose managers were convinced there was no way to reignite growth without resorting to price cutting.

In part, Nardelli won them over and energized them with his personal style of leadership. Deeply involved in all aspects of his business, he is curious and tireless—the personification of engagement. He never finishes a conversation without summarizing the actions to be taken.

He also made his vision credible by breaking it down into bite-size successes. He got previously aloof managers to get together with the decision-makers at the utilities and other customers to learn firsthand how they could enlarge Power Systems' share of the customer's wallet. He guided them into developing new value propositions, customer by customer and account by account, and they came to see possibilities they'd never previously imagined. Managers who used to dread meetings found themselves looking forward to them, because meetings at Power Systems had become forums for action and personal growth.

They're Decisive on Tough Issues

Decisiveness is the ability to make difficult decisions swiftly and well, and act on them. Organizations are filled with people who dance around decisions without ever making them. Some leaders simply do not have the emotional fortitude to confront the tough ones. When they don't, everybody in the business knows they are wavering, procrastinating, and avoiding reality.

Suppose, for example, somebody comes in for an appropriation to build a new plant, in a business where you're generally doing well. But the economy is going into recession. You have to ask whether this is the right time to build, or whether it makes more sense to outsource. Choosing to outsource will upset good managers and make you unpopular—your people would much rather have their own plant, and in this case they have good long-term justification for it. But you know building at this time would be a mistake, so you have to make the tough decision.

Or suppose someone you really like isn't cutting the mustard. Few tough issues are more challenging for indecisive leaders than dealing with people they've promoted who are not performing.

RAM: In January 2002, a company I work with was wrestling painfully with problems caused by indecisiveness at two different levels. As this book went to press, the outcome was still uncertain.

Ralph, a twenty-year veteran with the company, was promoted in January 2001 to president of the division. In the minds of the board and the CEO, this job would be Ralph's penultimate step before becoming CEO in 2003. The performance of his division was critical to the company's profits and price-earnings ratio, and was determined heavily by the energy and focus of its sales staff. But things were not going well. Critical sales territories were left uncovered because John, the executive vice president for sales, was slow to fill empty slots. John got the job because he was the CEO's executive assistant for two years. He had been identified as one of the company's high-potential people, and the CEO had promised him a key line job.

From the start, Ralph had qualms about whether John could do the job, because he felt that the man was indecisive and not an energizer. Each time Ralph talked to the CEO about his concerns, he was urged to be patient and give John time to develop. With the decision about John in limbo, the division's performance was suffering—and threatening the company's prospects. Competitors were gaining market share, and the industry was consolidating. If the indecisiveness continued much longer, the company would become a takeover candidate.

They Get Things Done Through Others

Getting things done through others is a fundamental leadership skill. Indeed, if you can't do it, you're not leading. Yet how many leaders do you see who cannot? Some smother their people, blocking their initiative and creativity. They're the micromanagers, insecure leaders who can't trust others to get it right because they don't know how to calibrate them and monitor their performance. They wind up making all of the key decisions about details themselves, so they don't have time to deal with the larger issues they should be focusing on, or respond to the surprises that inevitably come along. Others abandon their people. They believe wholeheartedly in delegating: let people grow on their own, sink or swim, empower themselves. They explain the challenge (sometimes at such a high level of abstraction that it amounts to superficiality) and toss the ball entirely into their people's court. They don't set milestones, and they don't follow through. Then, when things don't get done as expected, they're frustrated. Both types reduce the capabilities of their organizations.

Some people are just temperamentally unable to work well with others.

LARRY: I think I've got a good record of hiring people, but I've made my mistakes. For example, we hired a man I'll call Jim as a vice president in a staff advisory role. We were all extremely impressed with him. He was smart, articulate, and extremely appealing in the way he worked with his superiors. After a year, we put him in charge of a major business unit. But a year later the unit was in trouble. He didn't get new products launched in time, he was losing market share, and productivity was dropping.

When we appraised his performance, we discovered that the people who worked for him couldn't stand him. He was abrasive—"almost a drill sergeant," in words of one executive who worked with him. He didn't include others in decision making. Over time a wide gap grew between him and his people, to the point where he could no longer lead them. We had to remove him, and it took his successor a year to get the unit back on track.

Leaders who can't work through others often end up putting in untold hours, and pushing everyone else to do the same. They're like Charlie, whom I mentioned in chapter 3. I'm always asking such people, "What did you get done, and is everybody else in the game?" In performance reviews, I've often had to tell some very smart eighty-hour-a-week people that they need to change their work habits, and that the eighty-hour week is actually a major weakness. People like this usually force their direct reports to be in the office or the plant with them on Saturdays, Sundays, and holidays. They run them ragged and drain the energy of everyone around them. I'll tell them, "You have to come in here less, but your performance can't change—it must be just as good as it is now. Learn how to get things done through others. Because if you can't get things done through others, ultimately you're going to sink or burn out." If they promote others on the basis of very long hours worked—which they will, because that's what impresses them—those people will have the same problem.

People who can't work with others reduce the capacities of their organizations. They don't get the full benefit of their people's talents, and they waste everybody's time, including their own.

They Follow Through

Follow-through is the cornerstone of execution, and every leader who's good at executing follows through religiously. Following through ensures that people are doing the things they committed to do, according to the agreed timetable. It exposes any lack of discipline and connection between ideas and actions, and forces the specificity that is essential to synchronize the moving parts of an organization. If people can't execute the plan because of changed circumstances, follow-through ensures they deal swiftly and creatively with the new conditions. GE's senior leaders, for example, follow up every Session C after ninety days—before Session S begins—with a 45-minute teleconference among the people involved with projects that take a long time to be completed.

Leaders can either follow through one-on-one (for example, Dick Brown's "after-school" sessions, discussed in chapter 3) or in group settings as a feedback method. In the group, everybody learns something. The variety of viewpoints raised helps people see the criteria for the decisions, the judgments that are exercised, and the tradeoffs being made. This exposure calibrates people's judgments and aligns the team.

Never finish a meeting without clarifying what the follow-through will be, who will do it, when and how they will do it, what resources they will use, and how and when the next review will take place and with whom. And never launch an initiative unless you're personally committed to it and prepared to see it through until it's embedded in the DNA of an organization.

LARRY: Once I embrace an initiative, I make sure it's put into effect. If I let it wane after six months, wasting money and people's time, that's going to reduce my effectiveness in making future initiatives. People will think, "We'll give this three months, and ol' Larry will be off on something else," and their body language will show that they're skeptical. So I make a point of emphasizing that I'm committed and that we're going to do this. We may do it with or without everybody's support, but we're going to do it. Then people get the message quickly that this is not an experiment.

HOW TO GET THE RIGHT PEOPLE IN THE RIGHT JOBS

Traditional interviews aren't useful for spotting the qualities of leaders who execute. Too often they focus on the chronology of an individual's career development and the outline of specific assignments she's had. Interviewers don't usually dig into the person's record to see how she actually performed in her previous jobs. How, for example, did she set priorities? Did she include people in decision making? Can she justifiably take credit for those good financial results, or was she just moving from position to position one step ahead of calamity? There are far too many examples of people who have chalked up an admirable record by the numbers at the expense of people and then left behind a weakened organization. They jump ship at the right time, and their successors have to clean up their mess. Even when interviewers check references, they often fail to get to the heart of the matter.

When you interview, you have to create a full picture of the person in your mind based on things you can learn by probing them. Then you need to find out about their past and present accomplishments, how they think, and what drives their ambitions.

LARRY: Developing leaders begins with interviewing and assessing candidates. I'm not talking about overseeing the HR department and interviewing finalists; I'm talking about hands-on hiring. Most interview processes are deeply flawed. Some people interview well, and some people don't. A person who doesn't interview well may nonetheless be the best choice for the job. That's why it's so important to probe deeply, know what to listen for, and get supplemental data. It takes time and effort to drill down further, but it's always worth the trouble.

The first things I look for are energy and enthusiasm for execution. Does the candidate get excited by doing things, as opposed to talking about them? Has she brought that energy to everything she's done, starting with school? I don't care if she went to Princeton or to Podunk State; how well did she do there? Is her life full of achievement and accomplishment?

What does this person want to talk about? Does she talk about the thrill of getting things done, or does she keep wandering back to strategy or philosophy? Does she detail the obstacles that she had to overcome? Does she explain the roles played by the people assigned to her? Does she seem to have the ability to persuade and enlist others in a mission?

When I'm assessing an outside candidate, I want to verify his past. It's essential to talk directly to his references. When I arrived at AlliedSignal, I personally checked references for dozens of candidates. I remember fellow CEOs asking, "Why are *you* calling?" I'd answer that it was a personal concern of mine. If I'm going to hire someone, I don't want only human resources people checking him out; I want to check him out myself. And I don't talk to just one reference and leave the rest to HR; I try to talk with two or three, even if it takes a lot of time. You can't spend too much time on obtaining and developing the best people.

Many CEOs have told me that my reference calls were different from most because I focused so much on the candidate's energy, implementation, and accomplishments. I ask, "How does he set priorities? What qualities is he known for? Does he include people in decision making? What is his work ethic and his energy level?" Those types of questions get at the person's real potential.

When I make a call personally, I know I'm more likely to get a candid response. If I know the reference, I'll feel confident that I'm not getting any filtering. If I can't readily get a reference from a person I know, I don't want to hire the candidate. However, if you dig a little, you can always find someone in the evaluation process with a connection to the candidate.

I learned that lesson from a painful mistake I made early on at AlliedSignal. I had to let a senior marketing executive go not long after I'd hired him. He was a veritable windmill who spent his time pontificating and not getting anything done. As part of my follow-up after letting him go, I checked back with his references. One of them—someone I didn't know personally—said, "Well, he's had that problem all along." The reference hadn't told me about this man's problems before because he thought he had to fear potential liability.

The bottom line is that you have to be persistent in checking references and getting to the heart of the matter.

THE UNVARNISHED TRUTH

In most companies, assessing internal candidates suffers from the same general problems as assessing external candidates. The process is typically highly structured—in some cases, bureaucratic and mechanical. An executive who is preparing to evaluate a candidate gets guidance from binders prepared by staff people, which set out leadership criteria.

In reviewing a person's record, you have to get to the essentials of what makes the person effective in his or her job. What was his record of accomplishments, and how difficult were they to achieve? How effective was she in galvanizing the efforts of others and stimulating them to get things done?

One of the many things mechanical evaluations miss is *how* candidates performed in meeting their commitments—whether they did so in ways that strengthened their organizational and people capability as a whole or weakened it. *How* leaders meet their commitments is at least as important as *whether* they meet them and is often more important. Meeting them the wrong way can do enormous damage to an organization.

In a mechanical evaluation, it's simple to determine whether a candidate met his commitments: here are the targets he was assigned to meet, and here are the numbers that show whether he did or didn't. But what other circumstances affected his ability to meet them? Did he do a superb job in the face of adversity, or put the future of his business at risk in order to succeed in the short run? In meeting them, did he also strengthen his organization, giving people assignments that developed their leadership potential and gave them room for personal growth? Or did he leave behind a burnt-out and dysfunctional team? You won't find the answers to such questions on a checklist.

Meeting commitments the wrong way can sometimes have extreme consequences. Lucent and other telecommunications suppliers got into trouble when executives trying to reach ambitious revenue growth targets extended too much credit to one set of customers and agreed to take back products if the customers couldn't sell them.

But here's a more typical situation. Let's say Dave and Mike made their numbers last year but Sue missed hers. A mechanical—some would say objective—evaluation would indicate a bonus for Dave and Mike and none for Sue. But if you look more closely at the circumstances, you get a different outcome.

Dave coasted to success on a stronger-than-expected market. If he'd been doing his job well, he would have beaten the projections by 20 percent. At Sue's unit, however, profit plunged because a raw material shortage unexpectedly increased costs by 20 percent. The results would have been considerably worse if Sue hadn't quickly accelerated some planned productivity improvements. Her competitors in the industry missed their targets by even more.

As for Mike, he brought in the earnings he'd promised even though his business got hit as hard as Sue's. But he did it by halting the development of two new products and forcing a lot of product into the distribution pipeline—a situation that would harm the business by causing excess inventory in the next quarter. In other words, he borrowed from the future to make his numbers today.

If anybody should get a bonus, it's actually Sue. Yet time and again people are evaluated strictly on the numbers, or on what they think are objective criteria, and are rated accordingly. When the wrong people get rewarded, the whole organization loses. Problems don't get fixed, nonperformers get ahead, and the good performers start looking for jobs at places where their contributions will be recognized.

In a good evaluation, the leader looks closely at how the people under review met their commitments. Which people delivered consistently? Which ones were resourceful, enterprising, and creative in the face of adversity? Who had easy wins and didn't push for better results? And who met their commitments at the expense of the organization's morale and long-term performance?

Nowhere is candid dialogue more important than in the people process. If people can't speak forthrightly in evaluating others, then the evaluation is worthless—to the organization, and to the person who needs the feedback.

Most people we see, however, have *never* received an honest appraisal. It takes courage and emotional fortitude for those doing the appraisals to be forthright. More often a manager thinks, *If I sit down and tell this person she has a behavioral problem, that's a confrontational discussion, and I don't want to have that with her.* Without guidance, practice, and support, moreover, many managers don't have enough confidence in their objective judgments to be critical.

Don Redlinger was director of HR at AlliedSignal until the merger with Honeywell, and then he returned to the same job at Honeywell in 2001. At the pre-Bossidy AlliedSignal, he recalls, "Performance appraisals were generally delightful experiences. I would sit down with somebody who worked for me and said, 'Gee, y'know Harry, you're just wonderful in these six things.' And then evasively, I'd say, 'Just think about how you communicate with people,' and 'Wouldn't it be nice if you could even improve this wonderful capability.' Everything was vague and positive, syrup but no citrus.

"What the evaluator *should* have been thinking is, *I can make this person a lot better if I tell her she's got a problem, and she fixes it.* If you sit down with your boss and your boss hasn't said something to you about your weaknesses, go back! Because otherwise you're not going to learn anything."

LARRY: I tell my leaders they have to do the assessments in their everyday common language and in their words—not in human-resource-professional lingo. They can bounce ideas off the HR person—I do that myself. I'll say, "Here's my appraisal. You see this person. Do you have a different view?" I'll consider any good ideas they have and make them part of my appraisal. But basically it is my responsibility. The recipient needs to feel it is me, not someone else, who decides, and that I care.

A good, candid assessment talks about the things a candidate does well and the things he or she must do better. It's that simple. It doesn't use words that don't say anything. It's very straightforward. It's specific. It's to the point. It's useful.

For example, if you are doing an assessment, you may tell the person, "You're ambitious, you're enthusiastic, and you work well with people. You're conceptual, you're analytical, and you're a team player. Now, what could you do better? One, you're not aggressive enough. You're indecisive. Your standards aren't high enough. You don't develop your organization the way we ask you to—you didn't promote enough people last year." You illustrate these points with specific observations that you have made.

Assessments also have to be done in the context of the person's job. At Honeywell, for example, our leaders have to constantly link people, operations, and strategy, so they look at a person's performance in each of these areas. If a man in operations is weak on strategy, say, that gets noted down as one of the things he has to work on.

The leader doing the assessment has to also indicate how she may remedy the person's shortcomings, if talking to him isn't enough: "We're going to get this person a coach," or "He needs another assignment to work on this deficiency." The leader commits herself to giving this help.

Then the leader sits down with the person and discusses the appraisal. If I'm doing the appraisal, at the end I'll say, "Now I'm going to give you the last line. You've heard what I think—what would you like to add to this?" He'll reply, and then I'll say, "Well then, we've agreed that these are the issues you've got to work on. Now, some of the problems may be in your DNA, and you may not necessarily be able to change them. But you can modify them, improve them." Finally, the person being appraised initials the document, saying in effect, "Okay, you've said some nice things about me. I appreciate it. I accept the fact I have these learning needs and that I will participate in seeing if I can overcome them in the days ahead."

Such assessments go on and on, with thousands of people, throughout the whole Honeywell organization. When I go to one of the businesses, I look at the evaluations of all the top leaders there and their direct reports—maybe fifty or seventy-five of them. I go through all the high-potential people who were previously moved there because of their progress and performance. I identify those who aren't performing, and decide what to do about them. I follow through with a five- or six-page memo to them individually. Then I go back six months later and review to see that those actions were taken.

If that approach cascades down through your organization as it's supposed to, it will change your workforce.

■ ■ ■

People who are not accustomed to giving candid appraisals will struggle with the process at first. "They'll resist," says Redlinger. "How do you get them to understand it? When we started, it was contentious and difficult. Sometimes you'd take an extreme position to get people's attention. Somebody would say, 'Old Harry's done wonderful things,' and the reaction might be, 'You're crazy. He's a bum. He's never delivered results. He's full of hot air.' We'd get into arguments about these people, but in the end everyone knew more about the person being appraised.

"The candid appraisals taught general managers to focus on the quality of their talent as a fundamental, competitive advantage. As they upgraded their organizations over time, it occurred to them that the businesses worked much better, they competed much more effectively with supertalent. And the character of the conversations changed. Instead of debating the quality and performance of individuals, they became more focused on how we can help so-and-so overcome this gap in knowledge or experience or capability, or where should we move him."

There's nothing sophisticated about the process of getting the right people in the right jobs. It's a matter of being systematic and consistent in interviewing and appraising people and developing them through useful feedback.

The three building blocks we have described in part 2 are the foundation for the three core processes of execution. If you have leaders with the right behavior, a culture that rewards execution, and a consistent system for getting the right people in the right jobs, the foundation is in place for operating and managing each of the core processes effectively.

PART III

THE THREE CORE PROCESSES OF EXECUTION

The People Process: Making the Link with Strategy and Operations

The people process is more important than either the strategy or operations processes. After all, it's the people of an organization who make judgments about how markets are changing, create strategies based on those judgments, and translate the strategies into operational realities. To put it simply and starkly: If you don't get the people process right, you will never fulfill the potential of your business.

A robust people process does three things. It evaluates individuals accurately and in depth. It provides a framework for identifying and developing the leadership talent—at all levels and of all kinds—the organization will need to execute its strategies down the road. And it fills the leadership pipeline that's the basis of a strong succession plan.

Very few companies accomplish all of these objectives well. One of the biggest shortcomings of the traditional people process is that it's backward-looking, focused on evaluating the jobs people are doing today. Far more important is whether the individuals can handle the jobs of *tomorrow*. We have seen many people who led business units well, sometimes even superbly, who did not have the capability to take the business to the next level. Too often companies wait until the financial results are in before making corrections in key leadership positions. By then, the damage is done. The results are lagging indicators; they record the past, and with a time delay to boot.

RAM: Such people process failures cost business untold billions of dollars. Here's an unusually clear example. Some years ago, the CEO of a $4 billion chemical company invested $250 million to build a plant in Indonesia. It was part of his strategy to shift resources from a slow-growing U.S. market to developing countries, and it made good sense. He put the project in the hands of his Brazilian plant manager, who'd been doing an excellent job there. Early in 2001 the CEO called me and said, "Would you go to Indonesia? I've got this investment hanging around my neck like a millstone. Have a look at it." I went to Jakarta, where I discovered that the situation was hopeless. The plant's opening was way behind schedule because of construction delays. The manager couldn't handle the contractors, get licenses, deal with the unions, or recruit the people he needed. When the plant was finally running, he wasn't able to sell what he produced.

This manager did not have enough bandwidth to run a total business. That had been true in his home country of Brazil and was even more here in Indonesia, about which he knew little, especially how business gets done there. Yes, the man had run the Brazilian plant very well, but he was a technical professional, not a general manager. He did not understand the ins and outs of relationships with customers, markets, pricing, and the relationships you have to develop and maintain with various government authorities in a country like Indonesia. He had no ability to move in political circles—a prerequisite for doing business there. He did not see the total picture and did not have the full measure of how a business makes money, which is the heart of the skill known as business acumen. He was naïve as a businessman and didn't know how to pick the right local people. And there was no real contact between him and headquarters—where nobody knew anything about Indonesia either. None of the top twenty executives had been there, even on vacation. They got their location advice from a U.S. consulting firm, which didn't do anything to prepare them for the realities of doing business there.

How could the company have poured a quarter of a billion dollars into Indonesia without ensuring that its people knew how to run a business there? The CEO had picked this manager on the theory that they needed someone with strong technical strengths, and that somebody from one developing country would be able to handle another developing country. He didn't have a people process that yielded information about the man's leadership qualities or business acumen.

These kinds of decisions—putting the wrong people in place to execute a key part of a business's strategy—are common. Whether they're expanding abroad or launching a new domestic plan, far too many leaders don't ask the most basic questions: Who are the people who are going to execute that strategy, and can they do it?

The strategy was all right by itself, but the company had no hope of executing it. When I returned to the United States, I told the CEO that he had to write off the investment. Eventually he gave up on Indonesia and swapped that plant for one in another country.

Contrast this with people selection at another U.S-based company with overseas businesses. The company, the third largest in its field, has done very well for its shareholders; over the past decade its stock has commanded a 25 percent premium over the S&P 500. It's no coincidence that it also captures talent information on a global database.

In 1997 it faced a critical people selection issue. Its performance in Europe had been disappointing. Each country was a barony unto itself, and the company's European strategy was an unsuccessful summation of each country's strategy. The then-current CEO of Europe was about to retire after failing to achieve any synergies among the baronies.

Europe clearly needed a leader who could unite the businesses under a pan-European strategy and execute it with energy. The person who succeeded would be a prime candidate to run the whole company. So the criteria for the right person were rigorous: He or she would need breadth and depth, along with the ability to see external changes and link them with the business's activities, to build a new management fast and in depth, and to conceive and execute a vigorous strategy.

Traditionally, the pool of people for this job came from the U.S. or—to a lesser degree—from Europe. There was nobody in this pool who met the criteria. But as the discussions evolved, the global database turned up an unlikely possibility. A leader in a developing company—born and raised there—had risen to head the country's operations and had succeeded over the previous three years beyond anybody's anticipation. In many if not most companies, this man wouldn't even have been on the radar screen—they would have gone scouting for an outside candidate. But after thorough consideration, he was tapped for the European job. He succeeded there, too, and as of early 2002 was a strong candidate to become the company's CEO.

■ ■ ■

Identifying the match between the right person and the right job is not always as clear-cut as in the case above. Sometimes it means replacing an excellent performer with a person who is better equipped to take the business to the next level.

RAM: For example, the manager of a key division at a major company took the business from third place to first in its industry, worldwide, between the late 1980s and late 1990s. He globalized it, added services to its product offerings, and increased its productivity dramatically. Few people in the company had ever been better at execution.

But in a strategy session, the company's senior leadership concluded that future revenue growth would depend on an imaginative and broader redefinition of market needs, and faster development of products that used new technologies to commanding premium pricing. Linking the strategic requirements to the dialogues of the people process, the CEO came to the conclusion that despite the manager's unparalleled accomplishments, the division couldn't reach this next level without a new leader and management team.

The decision was a blow to the manager. But the company made the transition over several months, giving him time and support as he searched for a new job. He landed a great job, one that was a match for his abilities, in another company before resigning. And looking back three years later, the CEO's judgment was right. The new team has delivered annual growth of 15 percent in revenues and 18 percent in profits.

Sometimes the problem is clear but should have been avoided with earlier action. As we've noted before, a leader who achieves his numbers at the expense of the organization can do a great deal of damage. We know of executives who had to be removed because their negative behavior prevented their teams from working together effectively and drained energy from the entire organization. It's not hard to identify the person who is wrong for a job because of his behavior. But it's better to make sure such a person doesn't rise to a critical job in the first place. Early feedback on behavior can have a major impact on your competitiveness.

In many organizations, to create the discipline of execution, changes in behavior are needed at even the highest levels. Just a few years ago I was working at a major railroad company where the behavior of the executive vice president had an incredibly negative impact on the corporation. Socially, the man—I'll call him Jones—was charming. In the office, however, he was a terror, a rigid autocrat who cursed people out on an intercom that was connected to several offices in different locations over several states. Everyone knew he violated one recently reaffirmed value: respect for the individual. Because he controlled 80 percent of the budget and employees, his power was enormous, and he had the ability to make or break careers.

It wasn't just his underlings and peers whom Jones roughed up. He was discourteous to his peers and the CEO. The CEO had left the company for a time earlier in his career and then returned before being named to the top job. Jones felt he should have gotten the job instead and therefore gave the CEO little respect. For his part, the CEO was a bright, decent, mild-mannered person who tried gently to change Jones's behavior but got nowhere.

He basically tolerated Jones because of the man's past contributions.

One day I attended the railroad's executive committee meeting. The CEO, in his own nice, polite way, was explaining that the executive committee had to meet certain performance targets that required a major cost restructuring largely in Jones's area of responsibility. Jones responded—to my amazement—with vulgar language and condescending behavior, telling the CEO in no uncertain terms that it absolutely could not be done. Jones had no fear of being fired because of the CEO's decency and mildness and because he thought the board would not support the CEO if he moved against him. Further, Jones felt, the company would be paralyzed if he were forced out. But the CEO pulled himself together and dealt with the issue by getting the board's buy-in, and in a month Jones was out. There was a deep sigh of relief in the company. Jones's direct report then took over, and as a result of the changed behavior and cost restructuring, the stock price doubled within four years.

Executives like Jones drain an organization of its energy, and prevent people from developing. Leaders who fail to rein them in aren't doing their jobs.

■ ■ ■

A robust people process provides a powerful framework for determining the organization's talent needs over time, and for planning actions that will meet those needs. It is based on the following building blocks:

- Linkage to the strategic plan and its near-, medium-, and long-term milestones and the operating plan target, including specific financial targets.

- Developing the leadership pipeline through continuous improvement, succession depth, and reducing retention risk.

- Deciding what to do about nonperformers.

- Transforming the mission and operations of HR.

BUILDING BLOCK ONE: LINKING PEOPLE TO STRATEGY AND OPERATIONS

The first building block of the people process is its linkage to strategic milestones over the near (0–2 years), medium (2–5 years), and long terms, as well as the operating plan targets. The business leaders create this linkage by making sure they have the right kinds and numbers of people to execute the strategy.

Consider XYZ Co., which produces components for airplane manufacturers. Its new strategy calls for providing not just products but solutions, including post-sale services that will help retain customers and create annuity income. It also proposes to win nonairline customers. The dialogue in the people process zeroes in on the shift in skill mix that will be required for the new solutions-selling environment. The company has many people who are very good at what they do. But to execute the new strategy, it will need to reevaluate its leadership team and acquire fresh sales talent. Whose skills will become obsolete? How much lead time will it take to train engineers for the new mission of solution designs, and who will be accountable?

Determining that some of an organization's high performers can't handle the challenges of a new strategic future is a difficult social process—who wants to tell good people they aren't capable of moving to the next level? But it has to be done, and the kind of people process we are describing forces leaders to put these questions on the table.

Linking people, strategy, and operations also helps distill organizational challenges for the coming year. XYZ needs to improve supply-chain management, a crucial skill when selling services to an installed base. Besides new talent, this will require elevating aftermarket to a P&L center reporting directly to the president, so that it will have the focus and accountability it needs.

Strategy

Become the premier global provider of XYZ systems to a multiple class of customers.

Strategy Milestones

NEAR TERM (0–2 YEARS)	MEDIUM TERM (2–5 YEARS)	LONG TERM (5+ YEARS)
• Expand beyond existing product line toward selling solutions	• Further expand penetration in existing customer segments	• Become pioneers of leapfrog technology
• Launch new initiative to expand services to installed base	• Develop intermediate approaches to selling solutions to new customer segments	• Build more useful alliances
• Secure new expertise in technology	• Evaluate and engage alliance partners	• Develop low-cost sourcing ideas

BUILDING BLOCK TWO: DEVELOPING THE LEADERSHIP PIPELINE THROUGH CONTINUOUS IMPROVEMENT, SUCCESSION DEPTH, AND REDUCING RETENTION RISK

Meeting medium- and long-term milestones greatly depends on having a pipeline of promising and promotable leaders. You need to assess them today, and decide what each leader needs to do to become ready to take on larger responsibilities. The dialogue resulting from this assessment will reveal the adequacy of the leadership pipeline in terms of quality and quantity. Nothing is more important to an organization's competitive advantage.

THE LEADERSHIP ASSESSMENT SUMMARY: A useful tool in developing the total picture of the pipeline is the Leadership Assessment Summary (Figure 1). The summary compares both performance and behavior for a group of individuals. At XYZ, for example, it shows not only which sales executives win the big contracts (performance), but which ones collaborate with their peers and which are lone wolves (behavior). Solutions selling clearly requires a team approach, so sales executives who cast themselves as heroic individualists will need to develop new patterns of behavior to succeed in the new environment.

The Leadership Assessment Summary gives an overview of those in the group who have high potential and those who are promotable; those who have both qualities are placed in the upper-right-hand quadrant. Similarly, it shows who exceed standards in terms of performance but need improvement in behavior, as well as those who are below standard in both areas. The Leadership Assessment Summary is the bottom line and end result of several

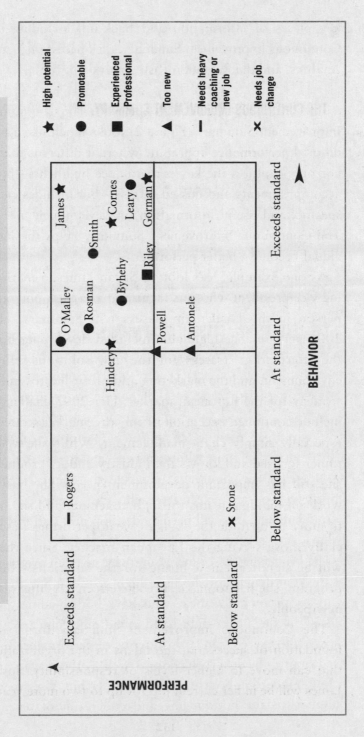

FIGURE 1: LEADERSHIP ASSESSMENT SUMMARY

High potential ★

Promotable ●

Experienced Professional ■

Too new ◀

Needs heavy coaching or new job |

Needs job change ✕

PERFORMANCE

Exceeds standard

At standard

Below standard

BEHAVIOR

Below standard   At standard   Exceeds standard

— Rogers

● O'Malley

★ Hindery

★ Rosman

● Byhehy

◀ Powell

◀ Antonele

✕ Stone

★ James

● Smith

● Cornes

● Leary

■ Riley

★ Gorman

151

key pieces of information and back-up, including the Continuous Improvement Summary, the Succession Depth Analysis, and the Retention Risk Analysis.

THE CONTINUOUS IMPROVEMENT SUMMARY: The Continuous Improvement Summary (Figure 2) looks much like a traditional performance appraisal. Where it differs is that it not only captures the key performance highlights—both accomplishments and missed targets—but includes clear, specific, and useful information on development needs. The Continuous Improvement Summary helps the individual become a better performer.

As one example, let's look at Susan James, a marketing vice president who was identified as a high-potential person in the Leadership Assessment Summary. Her 2001 performance highlights included developing both the aftermarket strategy for the new solutions-selling environment, and the marketing and profit-improvement strategy for the European market. Her 2002 challenges include continued execution of the aftermarket strategy, especially supply chain management. While she's customer focused and knows the industry and its products, she still has important development needs. She has to work on building teams through coaching, and she has to move to upgrade the skills of weak performers, especially those serving the European market. Since there will be significant new hiring for the solutions-selling program, she has to make sure she effectively integrates new people.

The Continuous Improvement Summary forms the foundation of succession, the talent in the organization that can move to higher levels of responsibility. Susan James will be in her current job for up to two more years;

Employee Name: Susan James, Marketing, VP   SUCCESS, ATTRIBUTES, AND BEHAVIORS

SKILLS	EXCELLENT	AT STANDARD	BELOW STANDARD
Bus. Acumen	•		
Cust. Focus		•	
Strategic Insight	•		
Vision and Purpose	•		
Values and Ethics	•		
Action	•		
Commitment	•		
Teamwork		•	
Innovation		•	
Staffing		•	
Developing People		•	
Performance	•		

RESULTS OVERVIEW

2001 PERFORMANCE HIGHLIGHTS

- Developed aftermarket strategy for solution-selling environment

- Developed marketing and profit improvement strategy for European market

2002 TARGETS MISSED

- Missed 2 major global accounts coverage in Hong Kong and France

- Did not recruit a Chinese marketing executive for greater China market

2001 CHALLENGES

- Continued execution of aftermarket strategy

SUMMARY STRENGHTS

- Extraordinary business insights

- Upholds the highest standards and sets right example

DEVELOPMENT NEEDS

- Needs to excel in recruiting staff

- Must devote energy to developing her people

- Move faster to upscale weak people

DEVELOPMENT PLAN

- Must work with a coach or mentor in the area of people skills

POTENTIAL NEXT MOVES (SHORT TERM 0–2 YRS)

- Stay in current role

POTENTIAL NEXT MOVES (LONG TERM 0–2 YRS)

- With significant improvement, she will be able to run a business unit.

she's definitely pegged as a "comer" who will be a division president in the very near future.

SUCCESSION DEPTH AND RETENTION RISK ANALYSIS: Analyzing succession depth and retention risk are the essence of talent planning and building a leadership pipeline of high-potential people. Taken together, they put meaning into the slogan "people are our most important asset" and are the foundation for discussing individual needs as well as lateral and upward job moves. They also focus on what needs to be done to retain critical people and replace those who leave unexpectedly, are promoted, or who fail.

The retention risk analysis looks at a person's marketability, her potential for mobility, and the risk a business faces if she leaves. If she's been in her existing job too long, she's likely to feel blocked from moving upward and hence susceptible to headhunter calls. Susan James, for example, is critical to the future of the business and its success in executing the new mission of solutions and aftermarket sales. XYZ will take several actions to retain her. It will give her immediate recognition and rewards for her accomplishments, and make sure she knows about the company's future plans. It will also give serious consideration to unblocking a higher-level position so she can continue to grow.

Succession depth analysis determines whether the company has enough high-potential people to fill key positions. It also looks at whether there are high-potential people in the wrong jobs and whether key people will be lost if a job is not unblocked for them.

The people process at companies like GE, Colgate, and Honeywell provide their bench strength. In the mid-1990s, when it had become clear that GE was the world's best producer of leadership talent, its division presidents were all retention risks. They were listed in the annual report and constantly circled by the top headhunters. GE's people process provided a forum for how to retain them by both gathering data and providing financial rewards such as stock grants that could not be cashed until retirement. When a key person does leave, however, the process almost always provides a needed replacement within 24 hours. For example, when Larry Johnson, the president of GE's appliance division, announced in spring 2001 that he was leaving to become CEO of the Albertson's chain, GE named his successor on the same day. It was also able to announce—on the same day—who would fill all positions created by the domino effect of related promotions.

Identifying high-potential and promotable people avoids two dangers. One is organizational inertia—keeping people in the same jobs for too long (a common practice in some industries). The other is moving people up too quickly (such as the twenty somethings at dot-com companies who didn't have the experience to handle senior management positions).

RAM: The tradeoffs between the need for succession depth, retention of future leaders, and meeting immediate economic realities can cause a great deal of trouble if a business doesn't have a strong leadership pipeline based on good information. One example of this recently took place in a large diversified company.

The company's second largest division, in terms of the profits it produced, had been on an expansion path. But business conditions had deteriorated—the industry's growth had turned negative, with little likelihood of an upturn for two or more years. The division president was due to retire in another year, and his successor would face tough challenges. Along with taking other cost-cutting measures, he would need to reorganize the division from P&L centers for each product line, each with its own marketing, legal, HR, finance, and engineering staffs, into a functional organization with central staffs.

There were two candidates for the job. Paul, forty years old and an extremely successful marketer who was popular with customers and colleagues, came from within the division and was considered a high-potential candidate for the CEO job within seven to eight years. Roger, in his mid-fifties, was a seasoned manager with a strong success record in two other divisions. With six years to go until retirement, he was not a CEO candidate.

The CEO strongly favored Paul. But the division president had developed doubts about the man as business conditions got tougher. Paul, he pointed out, had never held a P&L responsibility, and his evaluations raised doubts about whether he'd be tough enough to handle a situation that requires cost-cutting, resizing, negotiating with suppliers, and even repositioning the business. Roger, he felt, would be more likely to succeed—he'd handled several P&L responsibilities where he'd showed the ability to make the tough decisions.

But the CEO worried that the company would be blocking the succession pipeline if Roger got the job. Paul would most likely leave, and other talented people trying to move into the pipeline would have second thoughts about their future with the company. Moreover, he added, aspiring leaders in the pipeline might perceive the company as too risk averse if it chose Roger. "Let's test Paul," said the CEO. "He's so good, I think he'll grow into the job." The division president demurred. "If he *doesn't* rise to the job, we could have a disaster," he responded. "This division is crucial to the company's performance and Wall Street has gotten unforgiving. And honestly, I don't think he should be in the succession pool anyway."

The CEO and the group executive decided they needed more viewpoints. They brought in the CFO and the head of HR. The four debated—heatedly at times—for four hours. At the end they agreed that Paul was not the person for the job. The lengthy discussions revealed the flaw in his record of success. The record was accurate as far as it went. But he'd never had to face adverse conditions, and in exploring his personality traits, the group concluded that adversity was a test he would fail. What's more, they were persuaded that he should no longer be a potential CEO candidate.

The senior leadership team learned an important lesson from the experience. Having realized that they'd overestimated the abilities of someone seen as a high-potential CEO candidate, they went on to develop rigorous new criteria for the leadership pipeline.

TALENT REVIEW AT HONEYWELL

The talent review is the main social operating mechanism of the people process. At Honeywell, these reviews are called management resource reviews (MRRs). They are held in the spring and fall for two days, between the strategy and operations sessions. They are conducted throughout the organization, starting at the highest levels by the CEO and down in the business units by their general managers. They evaluate people in current jobs and those who are available to succeed them. They identify people who should be moved in the next year because of their potential. The talent review also talks about people who are not succeeding, and debates alternatives. Would coaching help them, or are they in the wrong jobs? The leaders have to show they have back-up candidates for people who might leave or be moved. Besides covering individual performances, the talent review also addresses organization design, general talent development, and skill gaps that the organization needs to fill in order to execute its strategy.

Honeywell's leaders spend a lot of time preparing for MRR meetings. They're responsible for their direct reports and for the direct reports of those people as well. They have to be ready not only to present their views but to discuss them—and to argue their case if others disagree. They're asked what they're doing to develop their people. Are those people growing and maturing? Why are poor performers doing badly, and what are the leaders doing about it? What have they been doing for each individual who's been promised help with development needs—did he or she get a coach, or another assignment to work out the deficiency?

Those attending the talent review meetings have to submit their assessments in writing a week before the meeting. The assessments that don't measure up are sent back for rework; maintaining the honesty of the process is mandatory.

LARRY: Why would an assessment be sent back? Maybe the words are lukewarm. The assessor says a person is doing "wonderfully," and under the heading for development needs he puts "none." Who is this manager kidding? The good Lord had some development needs. How can a leader help a person when he tells her she's got no development needs? I tell these people, "Go back and do the assessment you've been asked to do." Or an assessment might be perfectly candid, but the executive hasn't reviewed it with the person being assessed. That too is unacceptable.

Sometimes important issues are omitted in the assessments and then brought up in the meeting. Let's assume an individual's assessment listed under development needs is "indecisive, impetuous, doesn't listen." Then during the meeting, the person who submitted the assessment adds, "He's also got other behavior problems." Why weren't they on the sheet? How does the manager know about them? I tell him, "Don't talk to me about things that you haven't talked to him about. If he's got a behavior problem, put it on the sheet and have him acknowledge it."

An extremely important purpose of these meetings is to provide multiple viewpoints and judgments. Even the best leaders can't always rely on their own impressions. People struggle honestly with assessment out of concern that their views are apt to be subjective to some degree. But the dynamics of judgment change dramatically in a group. When several people who've watched the same person over time pool their observations in robust dialogue, subjective views become objective.

RAM: When it comes to talent reviews, you'd be amazed at how accurately, thoroughly, and quickly a group can pinpoint the critical issues. At one company I advise, the senior executive was meeting with a group to consider Walt, a thirty-four-year-old marketing vice president, for a job in operations. Walt was smart, personable, high-energy, and honest. He spoke eloquently. The board loved him, and he was on the short list of candidates to be groomed for succession to CEO. The CEO himself felt

Walt was probably at the head of the list. The operating job would be an important step in that progression.

Several members of the group had observed Walt over time, and they had assessments from others down the line who had worked closely with him. As they discussed him, three behaviors emerged that hadn't been revealed in Walt's appraisals—and which the CEO hadn't really focused on. First, it turned out that while Walt was full of ideas, he didn't rigorously follow through on them; he left the execution to others. Second, he was so eager to win big orders that he would consistently ignore the capital investment implications that others would point out to him—a serious mistake in a company that was capital-intensive, with high debt and low profit margins. Finally, he loved to go after megaprojects, but he avoided smaller ones that would be more profitable and less capital intensive.

These were very specific behaviors, observed by line leaders who worked closely with the man—not "round words" or abstract checklist items. In less than twenty minutes, the executives—including the CEO—reached the conclusion that Walt needed further development and wasn't right either for the operating job or as a CEO candidate.

Get five people who know the person together in a room. Get them to open up, to share and argue their observations, and to reach a conclusion. The diagnosis will come from the convergence of their diverse views. There's the core of your robust people process.

LARRY: When I'm making an assessment, I may not be able to characterize my thoughts as clearly as I want to. If I expose them to the rest of my leadership group, the chances are they will distill that thought more accurately. For example, in one talent review group, four of us were assessing Will, an inspiring engineer we'd hired from outside three years before. He was the head of a business unit. From the data put before us by his leader, we went through the pluses: he was technically savvy, he understood customer satisfaction, he was open to suggestions, he was creative, people liked the environment that he created, and a host of other positive things. The negatives: one, he wasn't familiar enough with numbers and often fell short of results. Two, he was not business mature. He was basically mature, but not with business matters. Three, he continued to need good coaching. The take-away conclusion: Will had very good potential but needed development.

Well, we all mostly agreed except one man who said, "You know, Will's doing better in his financial results than you suggest he is. If you look at the situation, he's had to overcome a technical problem with a product and a field quality issue as well." We debated that for a few minutes. I said, "He hasn't made his commitments. Now, you said there are reasons for it and maybe you're right, but the fact is he hasn't. Let's work on this characteristic with him and see if we can help bring about improvement." The three of us agreed that Will's circumstances wouldn't change our judgment: everyone has unforeseen events that come along, and the people who ultimately succeed are those who overcome them.

The man who'd raised the issue didn't change his mind, but that's all right—we agreed to disagree. You don't always get agreement, but the more people you listen to, the better a composite you get.

After one of these talent review meetings, I write a letter to each of the participants, spelling out what they agreed to do about their people. These letters are feedback essential to talent planning and building the leadership pipeline. Here are examples of the kinds of comments I make, taken from past letters. (The names and jobs are changed). I make every effort to be as specific as possible and then follow through during the year.

- "You have 1,000 engineers and have identified only seven high potentials at Band 5 [a leadership position]. That is not enough! You must make something happen here with your map for development combined with a learning plan as well as external hiring."

- "John X—if he continues to improve as you describe, we will look at a Band 6 [a higher leadership position] later in the year, after the beta product is out. His people feel he plays his cards too close to the vest. It isn't wise to lead that way. Help him improve his self-confidence and be more open. Please stay close to John. Continue to work on the relationship. We want him to succeed."

- "Brad X—is in over his head. He must fix his structure and hasn't filled critical roles in operations fast enough, and consequently he's failing. Reduce his scope. Find a way to help him and get him the help he needs, at the same time that you keep him motivated."

- "I do not see your successor in your organization. You must develop your replacement. This is a worldwide, complicated, exciting business where we need the best people. As your business grows, some of your talent will be passed by. You must fill your pipeline now with more high-potential people and make opportunities for them. Work on your issues identified in the team effectiveness and, as an action, establish an ongoing team-building process."

- "Pete X—is responsive, not proactive. Give him candid feedback. He doesn't show the passion for the role we need."

- "Julie X—is close to burnout. She's been in a tough job. You must identify her successor and determine the best way to utilize her many talents."

- "Greg X—is more process- than results-oriented. We haven't seen the ability to pull through results. He is more knowledgeable than others but doesn't perform. His people standards are not high enough, and he isn't demanding. His leadership skills are underdeveloped. Make sure he gets some help."

- "Mark X—his results are impressive, but he must temper his ego. Be very direct about what he needs to do to improve."

- "Todd X—has nice leadership skills. The transition to Group Z hasn't been easy. I'm concerned you think he is a retention issue. He needs to know we would like to move him to a P&L role soon."

BUILDING BLOCK THREE: DEALING WITH NONPERFORMERS

Even the best people process doesn't always get the right people in the right jobs, and it can't make everybody into a good performer. Some managers have been promoted beyond their capabilities and need to be put in lesser jobs. Others just have to be moved out. The final test of a people process is how well it distinguishes between these two types, and how well leaders handle the painful actions they have to take.

LARRY: There's one thing that wakes you up in the deep of night after you make these selections. You've all discussed someone carefully, listened to all viewpoints, and reached a conclusion you all feel good about. But no matter how successful a person has been so far, every promotion is a new decision. You can't take it for granted that he's going to succeed in the next job.

Nonperforming people are essentially those who aren't meeting their established goals. They're unable on a regular basis to accomplish what they are responsible for. Or maybe they failed to exercise the leadership expected of them in a situation, or a host of other things. Suppose a leader has a labor problem and the employees want to unionize. It isn't necessarily the leader's issue that it happened, but he has to take a lead role in trying to keep his company union-free. If he fails to stand up and do that convincingly and articulately and persistently, and the plant gets unionized, that's nonperformance.

Their failures don't mean they're bad people. It just means they aren't performing at the level that is essential for the company's success. And you deal with them quickly and fairly. For example, Rob was a good manufacturing man, and we made him a plant manager. But after a year it became clear he was not up to the task. He hadn't fixed a bloated cost structure and hadn't filled critical roles of operation fast enough. We had to decide what to do about him.

We didn't want to let Rob go—he's technically sound and good with people. So we agreed to give him a different job where we thought he could be successful and then we'd see what his next step would be. We did that, and he's still there.

Another man, Sid, did a wonderful job in his part of the world. We knew we would need a new general manager there at some point, but it would not be him. He was great at sales, but not a people leader. So we were candid with him. We told him his strong suit was customer relations, not strategy or people or operations. He knows he'll never run the business, but he's still there and doing a good job.

Sometimes there's no way around it—you have to let people go. But again you do it as constructively as you can. Let's assume I made a mistake in hiring Doug—he just wasn't ever going to work out in any capacity. I could go to him and say, "Doug, you're fired. The results haven't been good. Get out of here." But if I did, he'd leave with a sour taste in his mouth. He'd deal with Honeywell somehow down the road in another job, and with people who are our customers or potential customers. It wouldn't do us any good if he had nothing but bad things to say about Honeywell.

Or I could call him in and say, "Hey, look, Doug. We both made a mistake here. I apparently didn't explain the job to you as well as I should have. You haven't done it well. We've got to make a change, and we've got to do it in a way that you come out of this thing fine. First of all, I'm going to give you a year's salary, because this is as much my fault as it is yours. Two, I'm not going to lie when someone asks me to recommend you; I'm going to tell them you did some things wrong. But I'm certainly not going to submerge you. And three, I'm going to find ways so you can hold your head with dignity."

Then he'd probably say, "Larry, I want to resign. I want to say that I prefer to do something else." I'd say, "We'll know that you didn't resign, but if you feel better that way, fine." Preserving the dignity of people who leave jobs is an important part of reinforcing the positive nature of the performance culture.

Sometimes people recognize before you do that they aren't up to a job. After I returned to Honeywell, I didn't waste any time increasing the pace at which the company was operating. The aftermath of September 11 made the need for speed especially urgent. One of the managers came to one of our leaders in October. He was in his late fifties, was a good person, and had been doing a good job. But he was not intense. He said, "I don't like this fast pace or the amount of corporate interference. I want to retire at the end of the year." When I was informed about the situation, I appreciated his honesty. I'd rather have a person say that than sit there and let the results deteriorate and tell him he should retire. I told him, "We've got a tough year ahead of us, and it isn't going to be predictable. We'll have to do some rigorous things. You're making the right decision, and we'll be very fair with you." And we were.

BUILDING BLOCK FOUR: LINKING HR TO BUSINESS RESULTS

If you're starting to think that human resources is less important in an execution culture, let us correct that impression. It's more important than ever but its role has to change radically. HR has to be integrated into the business processes. It has to be linked to strategy and operations, and to the assessments that the line people ultimately make about people. In this new role, HR becomes recruitment-oriented and a far more powerful force for advancing the organization than it was in its typical staff function.

As Don Redlinger, the senior vice president of HR at Honeywell International, explains, "The paradox in working for somebody like Bossidy is that he's the CFO and the chief human resources officer and the chief strategist, but he has such a systemic view of how you make an organization perform that human resources people prosper in that environment. He demands that the organization use all of its capabilities to make money. He says all the things to us in HR that he would to a marketing person: 'I want bigger margins than anybody else, and to accomplish this we have to have great people and train them better and faster than everybody else. We need to have educational programs that are focused on key business issues and problems, the things that matter. HR's role is to help me solve these problems.'

"One of the first things Larry did when he got to AlliedSignal was to focus a lot on human resources talent. The HR function was one of the first elements of the organization we really drove to upgrade. And it gave us leverage all over the place.

"Things were different earlier in my career. Managers would assign HR people to recruit or to execute specific elements of a plan. For example, when they wanted to shut a plant down, you'd negotiate with the union. The nature of the HR beast today is very different. We're expected to come to the party with a point of view about how you achieve a business objective or a strategic plan, and we have a role that's very analogous to the role of a CFO or any other participant in the management process. The HR person not only has to be well trained in the craft—how to teach people, develop them, make them interested in staying with us, and know what's important for building momentum and morale in an organization, all of those tactical skills—but also must have the same characteristics as any business leader has. These include business acumen, the ability to understand how a company makes money, the ability to think critically, a passion for results, and the ability to link strategy and execution."

The number of companies that have strong, results-oriented human resources staffs is still small, but it's growing. At Baxter International, for example, HR is central both to a rigorous process for assessing, developing, and promoting people and to the company's strategic planning.

Baxter is a global healthcare company specializing in critical therapies for people with life-threatening conditions. The company aims to double its $7 billion in revenues over the next decade by leveraging and expanding its portfolio of biologics, pharmaceuticals, medical devices, information, and services. Having the right people in the right jobs is critical to its strategy. CEO Harry M. Jansen Kraemer, Jr., spent the late 1990s (when he was CFO) restructuring the company by selling off its slow-growth businesses and getting its finances in order. When he was named CEO in 1999, he made the people process one of his three top priorities (the other two: focusing on customers and patients, and providing a superior return to investors). Kraemer and his direct reports, who constitute the Executive Management Team (EMT), are deeply involved in people selection and development, and the company's strategic, operating, and people processes are tightly linked.

Baxter's growth planners, line executives, and HR people work together to identify the specific capabilities and skills the company will need to execute its strategies over the next several years. For example, says Mike Tucker, senior vice president for HR, "Through our strategic growth planning process during 2001, we identified expertise in regulatory issues, reimbursement, and strategic clinical marketing as organization capabilities we need to enhance and build. We then established teams to flesh out the details of exactly what was needed, what capabilities we currently had, and what we needed to do to fill the gaps."

Line people headed the teams: the head of Baxter's quality organization led the reimbursement initiative, the head of government affairs led the regulatory effort, and a marketing vice president led the marketing effort. Not incidentally, the leadership gave the executives valuable experience in leading cross-business, cross-geographic teams.

Identifying and filling critical jobs is a key part of Baxter's strategy process. In an annual half-day review, line executives, their HR vice presidents, Kraemer, and Tucker identify strategically critical positions in business units, regions, and functions, and make sure the right people are in these jobs. But the review is only part of the process; on this and other important issues, Kraemer and Tucker talk informally and frequently with each other and with the business and functional leaders and their HR leaders.

Critical jobs aren't necessarily high-level ones. "They could be four layers down in the organization," says Tucker. "For example, one might be somebody leading a clinical trial of a product where approval is critical to your strategy over the next three years. We'll say, 'Okay, based on where the renal business is going over the next three years, what are the key things the strategy has to deliver, and which jobs are critical to executing them?' Then we assess the incumbent against that skill set that's required. The logic here is that if we've got positions that are critical to the strategy execution over the next three to five years, we need our best people in them. They must be identified now since the jobs are too important for us to wait and develop someone for them.

"It forces executives to really drill down and identify what the critical jobs are. The first year we asked managers to identify critical jobs, everybody named all of their direct reports. We had to say, 'Wait a minute. Yes, your vice president of sales is very important, but she may not be critical to the execution of your new strategy.'

"When we consider whether a person is right for their job, we place them in one of three categories: a good fit, a stretch, or an action required. If the person is a good fit, we just stay on top and monitor her progress. If the person is a stretch, it means we're comfortable that he can deliver, but we might need to shore him up: maybe he's not strong on finances, so let's make sure we get a good controller for him and provide the organizational support necessary. If the person is an action required, it means that the person needs to come out of that position and leave the company, or else take a different job in the organization that she can handle. We hold the line executive in charge accountable for addressing the issue within six months."

"Senior slating"—choosing candidates for the roughly 325 vice presidential positions—is the showcase of Baxter's new people process. "Because it's so visible, it's really helped turn our culture around," says Tucker. Every Thursday Tucker sends a voice-mail to each of the top 150 people in the company, letting them know who has left the organization, which vice presidential positions are open, and which people have filled previously open ones. He spells out the job and candidate criteria for the open slots so the leaders can generate names for senior slating. (They can put themselves up, if they want to.)

Senior HR executives discuss the candidates at their weekly conference call the following Monday and compile an initial slate. "We might have fifteen names," says Tucker, "and they'll go through and pare it down until they come up with a short list of those they feel are most appropriate. We have to put on our company hat in these meetings. Somebody will say, for example, 'Well, we agree that Steve is a strong candidate, but his line manager's reluctant to make him available because he's really needed where he is.' We have to say, 'I hear you, but this job is more important from the company's standpoint, and we ought to make him available.' On the flip side of the coin, we might have to say, 'I know that you guys think this person ought to go in there. But we just can't afford to have her move.'"

Vice presidents with open positions work from this slate over the next two or three days, gathering information and feedback for making assessments before making their recommendations. Tucker then takes the final slate to the next weekly EMT meeting, where it's the first item on the agenda.

"The process has really speeded up slating," says Tucker. "Before we started in 1999, it took us on average about sixteen weeks to fill a vice presidential position. After the second quarter this year, we're down to seven because we're much more efficient. We've got a lot of discipline there. We follow up on it weekly. We move right through it. And the quality and breadth of the candidates is much better. It used to be that the same five names came up for every position.

"It's helped us in other ways. The executive management team has a much better knowledge of the top 150 to 300 people in the company, because those are the names that are coming up as candidates. And it's helped me to open up my own lines of communication. Those voicemails I send out get sent throughout the organization. As I travel around and go into a plant or office, I'll introduce myself. And somebody will say, 'Oh yes, you're the man who leaves the voice-mail.' So it's helped create the open communication style that we're trying to foster."

CANDID DIALOGUE: THE "LIVE AMMO"

There's no one system for creating and maintaining a robust people process, but certain rules are needed: integrity, honesty, a common approach, common language, and frequency. Above all, candid dialogue is critical. It's what Duke Energy's vice president of human resources, Chris Rolfe, calls the "live ammo" in the people process. It is fundamentally the social software of the people process.

Duke is a $49 billion (as of the end of 2000) producer, transporter, and manager of diverse energy sources. Like Baxter, Duke had to head into a new strategic direction after deregulation of the power business in the 1990s made its old utility model obsolete. Just from generating and selling power, Duke gradually developed a strategy that includes a mixture of physical assets such as power plants and pipelines, buying and selling natural gas and electricity on the marketplace, and financial operations such as risk management.

Achieving the new model required a new mix of people. Says Rolfe, "When our chairman, Rick Priory, asked us to do our first companywide assessment in early 1998, we could see we didn't have all the talent we needed to execute the strategy—and maybe not to beat some of our fiercest competitors. In general, the DNA of the people who can execute the new model is fundamentally different from the DNA of people who run a regulated monopoly. Certainly there's an operational component, but there are also tremendous financial components, merchant components, risk assessment and marketing components."

In 1999 Duke began to build a new people process. "One of the first questions was, what would the process look like?" says Rolfe. "We went through a pretty rigorous process of defining competencies. We started talking with a small group of our executives to build a framework for evaluating. Then we gave a validation test to our top five hundred executives and came out with correlations on these competencies, basically as high as the third-party firm who advised us had ever seen—that is, these were accurate predictors of business success in the new business model. We call this people-development-and-assessment model 'the successful executive at Duke.'"

The Duke team identified four basic groups of competencies: functional skills, business skills, management skills, and leadership skills. For example, says Rolfe (who was an engineer before moving into human resources), "Let's say Duke is considering hiring me as an HR executive. I have to have technical HR background—knowing ERISA, staffing, training, compensation, and such. These are functional skills. I have to have business skills too, like understanding Duke's business model and how it makes money. Three, I have to be able to manage. Management skills are an important criterion at Duke, because the operations leg of our model means management, planning, organizing, directing, and controlling work. Finally there are the leadership skills: Duke would ask, 'Does Chris have the fundamental leadership capabilities to be a senior executive at this enterprise?'

"It took us about a year to assess our people against these groups of competencies. What we came out with, beyond assessment tools and those types of things, was what I call a common language, a common way of talking about people. So now we don't just say 'He's a good guy' or 'She's really smart'—we say, 'We don't see in this person the ability to operationalize,' or 'That person is primarily operational and doesn't seem to have the strategic perspective.' "

Because Duke is largely decentralized, Rolfe centralized only three components of the human resources process—compensation for the approximately top two hundred people, domestic benefits, and a global Web-based HR data system. "We tried to get some of the rigor, for example, of a GE Session C, but with a less systematic, standardized, one-size-fits-all approach, because of our different governance model. The data system is critical for that rigor, and we spent a lot of time and money on it. Very few companies have one system for the entire enterprise, particularly those that have done a series of mergers and acquisitions. But when I talked to companies like GE, they told me, 'Above all else, you'd better get that piece right, because the fundamental question is, who works here? And without one global system, you cannot answer that question.' "

One benefit of the system is its usefulness in succession planning. "We began populating a global database of executive CVs. It was a common system that linked into our payroll, equity, and security systems, so we could produce what I lovingly refer to as baseball cards—one eight-and-a-half-by-eleven, with pictures, compensation, personnel information, and assessments, for every senior executive. Now when we talk about someone, the data is right in front of us, and we're all talking from the same sheet of paper, with not just a name but degrees, career interests, developmental plans, associations, third-party assessments if we've got those things, what his or her current compensation is, what it has been.

"Managers also do what we call a retention assessment, which would be a three-by-three matrix of the criticalness of a particular individual's role and their assessment of whether they think she's going to stay over the next five years—low, medium, high. So if you were a lethargic human resources executive, for example, who probably wasn't going anywhere and was adding very little value to the company, you'd be a low risk of turnover. But if you were a hotshot financial MBA who could run a business and could be attractive to other companies, you'd be assessed as a high risk of turnover.

"So everywhere on the globe we have one approach, one system, computer-based, feeding into a common database. I call that getting rid of the tower of Babel. We are all on one page."

The system's hardware is only the foundation of the people process. The critical software—the "live ammo"—is in the dialogues of the organization, the process of observation to common criteria culminating in candid assessment and feedback.

"HR can build all these elaborate systems, but it takes the leader of the company to make it real—coupled in our case with the marketplace and a fundamental shortage of skills. Rick Priory taught the enterprise how to be brutally honest, and he started normalizing an understanding of—in his phrase—'what good looks like.' Say my boss turned in an assessment on me, and he said 'Chris walks on water' on each of these competencies. The chairman would say, 'I know Chris. He does not walk on water in any of these, for heaven's sake. In fact, he's barely competent in these two. He's average in these eight, and he's pretty good in these four.'

"Rick holds us to standards of performance that are as aggressive and accountable as I have seen. Compared with our peers, we have some of the better metrics around—return on equity, return on assets, earnings growth, and so on. But if you look at our bonus payments, we rank below average. How can that be? The answer is that we have a culture of accountability. Rick is so tough about delivering the numbers—in the right way, of course—that everybody knows that without the right people, you're just not going to get there. So I keep talking about 'live ammo' in the marketplace. There is so much pressure on people to perform that nice round words become a luxury you can't afford anymore."

The main social operating mechanism for Duke Energy is Priory's policy committee, which consists of him, the heads of the three major business segments, and the heads of the four major staff functions—legal, finance, administration, and risk. The group meets biweekly for a full day and talks formally about people and talent three or four times a year. But much of the work gets done in the biweekly meetings.

"It's much more ongoing and real-time," says Rolfe. "We're updating these plans every day because our organization is so dynamic. And because it's on a computer-based system, it all feeds into the new succession and talent assessment on the spot.

"Rick's collegial management style includes people in the committee holding one another mutually accountable. No politics, no BS, everyone's opinion is important. It's not a democracy, but they'll debate an issue, kick it around. And there's usually one or two folks who, no matter what the issue is—an acquisition, a divestiture, a business decision—will call a spade a spade. And that's the culture here."

This is the social software that makes the system at Duke Energy work. Rolfe ticks off the four elements: "One, a culture of accountability for high performance, which makes you demand the best individuals in your organization. Two, a leader who is not only willing but also ready to question an assessment. Three, a collegial culture among the top executives of the enterprise, where they hold each other mutually accountable to be reasonable and fair and will push back on one another, just as the chairman will push back. And four, giving me, as the head of HR, the right to push too, because I have a fundamentally different perspective because of the work I do. I'm not a small executive of the company, but I'm certainly not these folks' peers. But when I make an observation, everybody listens to me because it's not about rank. It's about the credibility and the perspective of the individual."

■ ■ ■

The right people are in the right jobs when information about individuals is collected constantly and leaders know the people, how they work together, and whether they deliver results—or fail to. It's the consistency of practice that develops expertise in appraising and choosing the right people. The people process begins with one-on-one assessments, but when developed and practiced as a total process, it becomes incredibly effective as an execution tool. We now turn our attention to the strategy process. It's related to the people process, above all, because strategy comes from the minds of people. If a company has the right people, in all likelihood its strategies will be in sync with the realities of the marketplace, the economy, and the competition.

CHAPTER 7

The Strategy Process: Making the Link with People and Operations

The basic goal of any strategy is simple enough: to win the customer's preference and create a sustainable competitive advantage, while leaving sufficient money on the table for shareholders. It defines a business's direction and positions it to move in that direction. Why, then, do so many strategies fail?

Few understand that a good strategic planning process also requires the utmost attention to the *hows* of executing the strategy. A robust strategy is not a compilation of numbers or what amounts to an astrological forecast when companies extrapolate numbers year by year for the next ten years. Its substance and detail must come from the minds of the people who are closest to the action and who understand their markets, their resources, and their strengths and weaknesses.

A contemporary strategic plan must be an action plan that business leaders can rely on to reach their business objectives. In creating it, you as a leader have to ask whether and how your organization can do the things that are needed to achieve its goals. Developing such a plan starts with identifying and defining the critical issues behind the strategy. How is your business positioned in the context of its business environment, including its market opportunities and threats, and its competitive advantages and disadvantages? Once you have developed the plan, you need to ask: How good are the assumptions upon which the plan hinges? What are the pluses and minuses of the alternatives? Do you have the organizational capability to execute the plan? What do you need to do in the near and medium terms to make the plan work in the long run? Can you adapt the plan to rapid changes in the business environment?

To have realism in your strategy you have to link it to your people process: Do you have the right people in place to execute the strategy? If not, how are you going to get them? You've got to link your strategic plan's specifics to your operating plan, so that the moving multiple parts of the organization are aligned to get you where you want to go.

THE IMPORTANCE OF THE HOWS

If a strategy does not address the hows, it is a candidate for failure. This is a mistake to which AT&T fell victim. When Michael Armstrong came in as CEO in 1997, the company's major source of profit was long-distance voice and data and, to a lesser but growing degree, wireless. AT&T's balance sheet was clean, its debt was low, and its stock price was around $44. But external conditions were changing. Long-distance rates were falling as new rivals entered the business. Wall Street was granting higher price/earnings ratios to dot-coms and cable companies, on the belief that they were positioned for much stronger growth.

Armstrong set out to create a strategy that would put his company into the new growth markets. AT&T's opportunity, he concluded, lay in offering customers one-stop shopping for information transmission services: long-distance and local voice and data, via both phone and Internet, and multimedia services requiring broadband. Offering these services, however, would require AT&T to have direct access to customers; but that access lay in the hands of the regional telephone companies that had been divested from ATT under the 1984 breakup of the old telephone monopoly. The company weighed several options, ranging from building its own local infrastructures in key metropolitan areas to buying cable companies.

The strategy that Armstrong shaped had four building blocks: (1) buying cable companies, to gain direct, physical access to consumers; (2) providing customers with bundled service, which would let AT&T claim a larger share of their communications wallet than its rivals could; (3) executing the moves fast enough to generate revenue growth that would offset the decline in long-distance revenues; and (4) relying on regulatory implementation of the 1996 Telecommunications Act, which was supposed to block local telecoms from competing in long distance until they opened their networks fully to long-distance carriers.

It was a highly appealing strategy. The security analysts bought into the idea, and the initial market response was positive. Yet the strategy failed utterly. In December 2001, the company sold the cable holdings, for which it had paid $100 billion, to Comcast for $44 billion in equity and the assumption of $25 billion in debt. The move left the company essentially where it was when it started, and AT&T stock was trading at around $18.

What went wrong? For the strategy to succeed, all four of the building blocks had to be sound. But all turned out to be based on faulty assumptions. AT&T Broadband was composed of two high-profile acquired cable companies, TCI and Media One, and some existing lines of business. The cable acquisitions were costly: AT&T paid top dollar for them and then some. At the same time, long-distance prices declined faster than assumed, and as they did, the company's stock price fell too. This made the acquisitions even costlier and added a huge amount of debt to the balance sheet. Consumers weren't as interested in bundled services as AT&T had expected, and the company did not market the proposition well or soon enough. It took AT&T much longer to execute its plan than it had anticipated. Finally, the regulators didn't enforce the Telecommunications Act as well as AT&T had hoped, which meant that the company took a double hit: local phone companies entered the long-distance market, and long-distance carriers got less local access than the plan presumed.

AT&T also made some critical people choices badly. Three sets of executives ran the cable businesses over a three-year period, none of them very effectively. The stock price was dealt another blow when major investors such as CalPERS (the retirement system for California public employees) and TIAA-CREF (the retirement system for teachers) voiced their dissatisfaction with execution at Broadband.

AT&T's strategy was disconnected from both external and internal realities. It didn't test its critical assumptions to see if they were robust, and it had no alternative plan for what to do if one or more of them proved wrong. The company did not take into account its organizational inability to compete against aggressive rivals in a fast-moving marketplace. Its culture, which was not much changed from the old monopoly days, could not execute well enough or fast enough to make the plan work soon enough.

THE BUILDING BLOCKS OF A STRATEGY

The substance of any strategy is summed up by its building blocks: the half-dozen or fewer key concepts and actions that define it. Pinpointing the building blocks forces leaders to be clear as they debate and discuss the strategy. It helps them judge whether the strategy is good or bad and why. It provides a basis for exploring alternatives if needed.

If the building blocks are clearly defined, the essence of even the most complex strategy can be expressed on one page. For example, in 1991 a $500 million business unit of an industrial company, a supplier to major auto manufacturers, was barely breaking even. Its product was considered a commodity and was under continued pricing pressure from its customers. The unit developed a new strategy based on three building blocks. The first was to lower costs by moving production out of the United States to a network of plants well positioned to serve both global customers and local markets. The second was to continually redesign the product to achieve technological differentiation, which would add value and command higher prices. The third was to create a new organizational structure staffed with carefully selected management teams. Marketing remained localized, but product development, technology, manufacturing, and finance were made into global organizations.

The unit executed all three of these building blocks simultaneously, and it achieved excellent margins and returns. Today it is the supplier of choice for the world's top ten automotive customers.

Throughout the process, the unit's leaders kept in touch with reality. For example, the original plan called for moving the technology program from the United States to a lower-cost country. But when American engineers balked at making the move, it abandoned this idea. The leaders also kept the strategy up to date, reviewing the plan three times a year and refining it as conditions changed.

■ ■ ■

The focus of this chapter is on business unit strategy, but it's important to understand the distinction between strategy at the business unit level and strategy at the corporate level.

Corporate-level strategy is the vehicle for allocating resources among all of the business units. But it should not be simply the sum of those parts. If it is, then the business units could do just as well standing on their own (or better, since they wouldn't bear the burden of corporate overhead). Corporate leaders must add value to strategies created at the business unit level. At GE, for example, the boundarylessness that Jack Welch introduced assures a constant exchange of ideas and best practices among diverse business managers, significantly multiplying the company's intellectual capital.

A corporate strategy also defines the walls of a company—the businesses it wants to be in and the general arena of play. Honeywell, for example, is an industrial company; consumer products won't play well in this arena, no matter how exciting they may be.

Corporate-level strategy analyzes the mix of businesses

and makes decisions about whether the mix should change in order to earn the best sustainable return on the company's capital. For example, GE exited the aerospace business when the Reagan presidency ended, anticipating the relative decline in defense expenditures and a fast consolidation of the industry. Jack Welch thought that financial and managerial resources would earn greater returns elsewhere. Strategic value is also added by initiatives to improve performance throughout the company, such as Six Sigma, digitization, and implementation of a good people process. GE's celebrated people process started as a Jack Welch initiative for human resources to produce a systematic way of assessing talent that would help develop future leaders. More recently, GE has formalized the search for GE "diamonds in the rough," people of substance who may not have the polish of some of their peers and who might get overlooked at other companies. They may be struggling in their current jobs because of circumstances they cannot control, such as working for a bad boss. The initiative will help move these people to better environments where they can grow and be ready to take on more responsibility in the future.

BUILDING THE STRATEGIC PLAN

When a business unit creates its strategy, it clearly lays out in specific terms the direction of the unit: where it is now, where it will be going it in the future, and how it will get there. It looks at the cost of the strategic results it wants to achieve in terms of the capital resources it needs, analyzes the risks that are involved, and instills flexibility in case new opportunities arise or the plan fails. The strategy statement elucidates the positioning of the business in the context of its market segment map and analyzes the strengths and weaknesses of competitors.

A business unit strategy should be less than fifty pages long and should be easy to understand. Its essence should be describable in one page in terms of its building blocks, as we've shown for AT&T and the automotive parts manufacturer. If you can't describe your strategy in twenty minutes, simply and in plain language, you haven't got a plan. "But," people may say, "I've got a complex strategy. It can't be reduced to a page." That's nonsense. That's not a complex strategy. It's a complex thought about the strategy. The strategy itself isn't complex. Every strategy ultimately boils down to a few simple building blocks.

LARRY: A good strategic plan is a set of directions you want to take. It's a roadmap, lightly filled in, so that it gives you plenty of room to maneuver. You get specific when you're deciding the action part of the plan, where you link it with people and operations.

Who Builds the Plan?

To be effective, a strategy has to be constructed and owned by those who will execute it, namely the line people. Staff people can help by collecting data and using analytical tools, but the business leaders must be in charge of developing the substance of the strategic plan.

They know the business environment and the organization's capabilities because they live with them. They're in the best position to introduce ideas; to know which ideas will work in their marketplace and which ones won't; to understand what new organizational capabilities may be needed; to weigh risks; to evaluate alternatives; and to resolve critical issues that planning should address but too often doesn't. Not everyone can learn to be a good strategic thinker, of course. But by working in a group, guided by a leader who has a comprehensive understanding of the business and its environment, and by using the robust dialogue that's central to the execution culture, they all can contribute something—and all will benefit from being part of the dialogue.

A good strategy process is one of the best devices to teach people about execution. It makes the mind better at detecting change; pieces of paper don't do that. People learn about the business and the external environment— not just data and facts, but how to analyze it and use judgment. How is the plan put together? How is it synchronized? They discover insights, and develop their judgments and intuition. They learn from mistakes: "Why, when we made our assumptions, did we not see the changes that overtook us?" Discussing these things creates excitement and alignment. In turn, the energy that these discussions build strengthens the process.

LARRY: The leader of a business has to own the strategy development. He doesn't have a strategic planner do all the work, then come in and introduce himself to the subject the day it's being presented. He takes responsibility for the construction of the plan and gets some help, and then—once everyone agrees with the strategy—he takes responsibility for developing action plans.

To start the planning process at Honeywell, I call the head of each unit, along with the strategic planner in his place and maybe one of the corporate staffers, and we get agreement on the critical issues confronting the plan. After the plan has been constructed, but before I review it at the corporate level, each leader will have reviewed that plan with his subordinates and gotten their input on it. After all, these are the people who will have to implement the plan.

QUESTIONS FOR A STRATEGIC PLAN

LARRY: The strategic plans for Honeywell's businesses give special attention to environment, competition, and why some companies in a particular business are more successful than others. A plan will start off with a database that talks about the health of the business's environment—is it a growth market or not? If the business is in an environment that is growing at, say, a 2 percent annual rate, it is not going to grow it much above that level unless it has a new product or strategy that is truly unique. The Honeywell automotive business, for example, is in a low-growth environment, so we are cautious about our expectations for it and the amount of resources we allocate to it.

The strategic plan then lays out the market share for that business, indicating whether it is in a leading or an insignificant position. Market share is the ultimate scorecard, and obviously it will influence the strategy. If the business's share is small and it is in a high-growth environment, the plan will lay out what it can do to improve market share. It will also detail whether the business has gained or lost market share in the past year.

The strategic plan also contains a short synopsis of the strengths and weaknesses of each major competitor to the business. People have to understand that the world isn't going to watch and wave while they do something—

competitors are going to do something too. In the Honeywell avionics business, the competitive analysis focuses on companies like Rockwell Collins and France's Thalen.

The plan then explores what kinds of companies are successful in the environment of that business. Are they low cost? Do they have innovative technologies, expansive distribution systems, a global footprint? In other words, what separates the successful companies from the other companies in the same industry?

You don't just put a plan together and then go back and see whether it can be of help to you. Decide on the objectives at the beginning: "What do we want to get done? What are the critical issues we need to understand better? Why at the end is it going to be helpful to us?" As you fill in the plan around those objectives, you've got a chance to accomplish something.

■ ■ ■

A strong strategic plan must address the following questions:

- What is the assessment of the external environment?

- How well do you understand the existing customers and markets?

- What is the best way to grow the business profitably, and what are the obstacles to growth?

- Who is the competition?

- Can the business execute the strategy?

- Are the short term and long term balanced?

- What are the important milestones for executing the plan?

- What are the critical issues facing the business?

- How will the business make money on a sustainable basis?

What Is the Assessment of the External Environment?

Every business operates within a shifting political, social, and macroeconomic context, and the strategic plan must explicitly state the external assumptions that management is making. The leaders of a business unit have to scrutinize its environment carefully and understand it well. They should examine everything from economic and demographic trends and regulatory shifts to new technologies, alliances between competitors, the drivers of increasing or decreasing demand for its products, and so forth. AT&T's assessment of its external environment failed to anticipate that regulators might not behave as it hoped, and that the capital market boom in dot-coms, telecommunications, and media might not remain strong.

The general environment is the same for every player. What differentiates the successful ones are their insights, perceptions, and abilities to detect patterns of change and relate them to their landscape, industries, competition, and business. For example, when the Asian contagion hit in 1997, most companies failed to detect the change until about March 1998. GE and AlliedSignal saw it before the end of 1997 and changed their 1998 operating plans, to be able to deliver the results they'd promised despite the new circumstances. Very few other companies responded adequately to the crisis.

How Well Do You Understand the Existing Customers and Markets?

Perhaps not as well as you think. When it comes to industrial customers, for example, the buying decision is more complex than just the customer's purchasing manager who negotiates prices. The division manager of a large industrial company recently proposed a growth strategy requiring a $300 million capital investment. The strategy would adapt an existing technology to a new product that would be sold to a new set of customers. The plan he proposed was elegant in the way it answered the usual strategy questions with data about the competition, the industry, and the external environment. The CEO listened patiently for twenty minutes, an unusually long period of time for him. However, he couldn't wait any longer to ask the following questions. First, who buys this product? The division manager answered that it was the purchasing managers of customer companies. The CEO said, "Really? Let me rephrase the question. Who specifies that this product should be purchased?" The division manager answered that it was obviously the engineers. The CEO's final question, delivered in a stern tone, was, "How many engineers did you talk to?" The dead silence meant that the project was rejected.

People tend to look at their businesses from the inside out—that is, they get so focused on making and selling their products that they lose awareness of the needs and buying behaviors of their customers.

The issue is simply understanding the specific people who make the purchasing decisions and their buying behavior. At large industrial companies, for example, engineers and purchasing agents usually do the buying. But in small companies, the CFO or even the CEO will be involved, because they have to pay close attention to cash flow. This requires taking a significantly different approach to the customer.

What Is the Best Way to Grow the Business Profitably, and What Are the Obstacles to Growth?

Does your business need to develop new products? Does it need to take existing ones into new channels and to new customers? Does it need to acquire other businesses? How are its costs compared with those of its competitors—and what productivity programs do you have in place to improve your cost position?

In the early 1990s, GE Medical, the medical systems business of GE, hit the wall in the United States. It experienced no growth because reimbursement policies were discouraging hospitals from buying new equipment. The business unit manager, John Trani, and his team developed a growth plan to move into adjacent segments and supply maintenance and other services to owners of medical equipment, whether sold by GE or by competitors. There were obstacles: some of the non–GE Medical equipment was far removed from GE Medical's own high-tech diagnostic machinery, and the unit would have to persuade potential customers that its proposition had value. The unit overcame the first obstacle by acquiring a company specializing in the lower-tech equipment that GE didn't make, and by focusing on process improvement to increase the productivity of its own people. It overcame the second by taking an entrepreneurial gamble on a small hospital in Ohio: it contracted to maintain all of the equipment and guaranteed the hospital that it would save money. Once it succeeded, GE Medical was able to go to potential customers with a track record. That original growth initiative shifted a steadily increasing portion of GE Medical's revenues into high-margin services with higher levels of cash flow.

One tool that's useful in defining growth opportunities is market segment mapping. The tool is simple enough; any business can be segmented. Many consumer goods companies use it to great advantage. But many more don't, and neither do all but a few industrial companies. Planners will talk about market segments, but fewer than 5 percent of the plans we've seen contain any useful mapping.

To understand how it works, let's look at A.T. Cross's segmentation of the luxury pen market. A simple map of Cross's market segments identifies three different consumers. The first is the individual who wants to buy such a pen for herself; the second is the person who buys one as a gift for another individual; and the third is the corporation that buys thousands, with its logo on them, and uses them as institutional gifts. For each market segment the product is essentially the same, but demand is different and so is the strategy. Each requires Cross to deal with different competitors, channels, economics, and pricing.

A new market segment in the aircraft industry has recently changed the dynamics for manufacturers and suppliers. In the past seven or eight years, as commercial airline service and schedules deteriorated and prices rose, the corporate jet business has taken off. In 1996 Executive Jets pioneered fractional ownership, which is time-sharing in the sky, with its NetJet program. The new segment it created rapidly became the fastest-growing one in the business. Among manufacturers the big winner was Bombardier of Canada, because Bombardier built planes that were right for the market—larger than the ones made by rivals such as Beech Aviation and Cessna and smaller than those of Boeing or McDonnell Douglas, and foreign competitors.

Who Is the Competition?

Sometimes businesses miss the emergence of new competitors who have more attractive value propositions for their customers. For example, while Staples, Office Depot, and OfficeMax were competing with one another, they failed to see the inroads that Wal-Mart was making into the discount office supplies market. All three have since been losing share, and their stock prices have declined as a result.

RAM: Most often companies underestimate their competitors' responses. One December I had a call from a CEO of a $5 billion company. He said, "I announced nine months ago that we'll show earnings of five dollars a share for the coming year. But the way things are going now, we won't do better than three-fifty. It's a good market, and demand is not declining. I'm very embarrassed."

We spent a day together, and here's what we learned. One key division was responsible for the company's failure to meet its earnings forecast. The person who was running it was brilliant and very interpersonal, a top scholar at Harvard Business School who'd worked for a leading consulting group. He'd been in this company five years. Though it hadn't been announced, he was generally understood to be the successor CEO.

His strategy was to gain market share by cutting prices. He'd been adding capacity over the past three years, which consumed a lot of cash since the industry is capital-intensive and has thin profit margins. He calculated that his increased volume from cutting prices would lower costs significantly. When the CEO reviewed it, the strategy made sense to him.

We went over all this and finally I asked, "So what did you miss?" By then the CEO had figured it out. "I did not ask him what the competitors' reaction would be," he said. The biggest competitor matched the price cuts almost immediately, and the others followed. Prices for the entire industry went down. The company had the largest share and got hurt the worst.

The CEO replaced the division head, and the new man he brought in gradually rolled the prices back up, initiated productivity programs, and reduced costs. The competitors followed the price increases, and by the end of the next year the CEO had made his $5 a share.

Sometimes people have the opposite problem—they *overestimate* the competition because they haven't asked the right questions, and they miss opportunities they should be grasping. For example, I was working with a small player in the software industry. Its product was

excellent—it's at the center of the bundle of software packages that enable appliances to connect with one another
and the Internet—but the company was going nowhere
with it. As I talked to its leaders, it emerged that they were
so terrified of Microsoft, they were pulling their punches.
Microsoft didn't have a competing product, but every
time they did an analysis of the competition, they would
say, "Once Microsoft hears about what we're doing,
they'll come after us with all of those resources." What
they didn't understand was that Microsoft actually had a
lousy record of execution in their area. They knew how to
execute. If this moved fast to get key initial customers who
would be references for other customers, they could take
firm control of the market.

The company went ahead and is now succeeding. To
execute still better, it is also changing its organizational
structure and changing key people in both sales and
design. It is refocusing the sales force to attack multiple
segments and improve cycle time.

Can the Business Execute the Strategy?

An astonishing number of strategies fail because leaders
don't make a realistic assessment of whether the organization can execute the plan. This was one of the problems
at Xerox, Lucent, and AT&T. Another example is Joe, the
CEO we talked about at the beginning of chapter 1—the
man could not understand why his carefully planned
strategy failed, and he was about to be fired as a result.
He and his leadership team would never have been in that
position if they had assessed their organization's capabilities. They would have found that it fell far short of being

able to execute the strategy. The top two layers of the leadership ranks did not have enough people who met their commitments. The manufacturing people didn't know how to improve process flow in their plants, which meant that the product didn't get out as it should have. Manufacturing also lacked continuous improvement processes, so they could not deliver the consistent cost and quality improvements that buyers expected. Finally, they had little capability to work with suppliers to reduce costs early in the supply chain (an issue for many manufacturing companies, by the way).

How do you make such an assessment in your business? In a sense, this shouldn't even be a question. If you're doing your job as a leader—if you're intimately involved in the three core processes, running the robust dialogues that permit candid assessments—you can't help but have an idea of your capabilities. But don't stop there. Listen to your customers and your suppliers. Get all your leaders to do the same, and ask them to report what they've heard. And don't forget the security analysts, who look at you sharply from the outside. Some are good, some aren't, but after a while you will know which ones you can learn from.

LARRY: You measure your organizational capability by asking the right questions. If your strategy requires a worldwide manufacturing capacity, for example, you need to ask: "Do we have people with global experience? Do we have people who know how to source? Do we have people who can run a supply chain that extends worldwide?" On a scale of one to ten, if your answers come up a six, you don't have enough capability.

If you have a mechanical engineering business that's going toward electronics (as most of them are), how much depth of people and experience in electronics do you have? Do you have capability in chip technology, or in information technology? If software is going to be embedded in the product, do you have enough software people? And if your answer is an eight or a seven, what do you need to do to get it to ten? Do you have people who understand Six Sigma, for example, and have achieved at least Five Sigma? Engineering organizations are often not on the cutting edge of their field's discipline. Can you put a new product in and expect that your people will step up to the bar and respond? If the answer is no, you need to search for new talent or take other corrective action, such as a marketing agreement with someone who can make the product. In finance, do you need a basic cost-accounting activity, or do you need a more sophisticated capability that can handle things you have to do globally, such as hedging?

You can certainly increase your capability—you're looking at it not just today but two years out. But what you distill and gain from the process is an understanding of what needs to be done.

What Are the Important Milestones for Executing the Plan?

Milestones bring reality to a strategic plan. If the business doesn't meet milestones as it executes the plan, leaders have to reconsider whether they've got the right strategy after all. In the Honeywell automotive business mentioned earlier, the short- and medium-term milestones were to develop programs to move to low-cost manufacturing locations, as well as to create and execute a technology map to differentiate the product and increase margins. The long-term (five-year-plus) mission was to position the business so that it could break out of the auto industry and adapt the technology to serve customers in other markets.

A good strategic plan is adaptable. Once-a-year planning can be dangerous, especially in short-cycle businesses where markets won't wait on your planning schedule. Periodic interim reviews can help you to understand what's happening and what turns in the road are going to be necessary. This is another reason your business leaders have been in on the plan from the beginning. Because they helped build it and they own it, they carry it around in their heads all the time—unlike a staff-driven planning book, which will spend a year on shelves before being discarded. So they can regularly test it against reality. And because you've crystallized the essence, it doesn't take too long to implement changes.

Are the Short Term and the Long Term Balanced?

Strategy planning needs to be conducted in real time, connected to shifts in the competitive environment and the business's own changing strengths and weaknesses. This means defining the mission in the short to medium term as well as in the long term. Breaking the mission down into these chunks will help bring reality to the plan—thinking about what will deliver results in the short and medium term will give you an anchor to build for the future.

Anything, from customer preferences to cash flows, can change in mere moments. Businesses have to prepare themselves to adapt to an economy of constant change. In developing your plan, you need to look ahead to landscapes that are more likely than not to change before your plan can come to fruition.

If, for example, you decide to move some of your plants to low-cost countries, it's not necessary to decide on which plants too far in advance. Opening a plant in, say, China may be attractive now, but a year from today it may not be the best alternative. The point is first to get the principle across—in this case, the need to reduce costs by moving some part of the operation to a new locale. Then make a concrete decision as you move closer to the date.

Balancing the short run with the long run is thus a critical part of a strategic plan. Most plans don't address what a company has to do between the time the plan is drawn up and the time it is supposed to yield peak results. A plan that doesn't deal with the near-term issues of costs, productivity, and people makes getting from here to there unacceptably risky—and often impossible.

LARRY: You can't just say *mañana*. You've got to have a plan that both plants seeds and harvests, that can make your financial objectives in the short term as well as do things that extend the life of the business in the longer term.

One manager, Jerry, introduced a plan that looked like a hockey stick: earnings initially dropped from the operating losses but then rose sharply. He said, "We're going to have flat earnings for three years while we get this strategy launched." I said to him, "Jerry, I can't have flat earnings for the *company* for three years, so who is going to make up the difference? If you want to engage in something that's got a substantial operating loss aspect to it, then it's incumbent upon you to explain how you're going to fill this so-called bathtub between now and when this project becomes profitable. If you can't overcome it, then the enthusiasm for investing in that project is diminished."

When you press people on this kind of issue and make it clear that you're not going to give them an earnings holiday while they get their project going, the amount of imagination and innovation that occurs is remarkable. Jerry came back and said, "I can take more profit out of this product line in the short term, because I don't think its long-term potential is that good anyway. And I can sell off a small business and make a profit, because I don't think it's the best business for us to be in. I can cut expenses by ten percent during this period as a way to generate more earnings. I can do four or five things that can overcome this loss from the new product."

One important result that comes out of this approach is that the whole business team owns the new project now. Since everybody's making some kind of contribution to support it, everybody is committed to it.

RAM: Intel mastered the art of balancing the short term and the long term from the time it was a $200 million company. They understood that to win in their game, they must invest in improving manufacturing processes and equipment ahead of the new-generation technology, so that it can be tested. That way they are ready for the next generation, thus meeting short-term goals and also building for the longer run.

Achieving this balance requires creativity and idea generation, finding resources outside the corporation if necessary for the long term. That's common now in the pharmaceutical industry. Warner-Lambert, in developing the cholesterol-lowering drug Lipitor, needed resources as well as more extensive sales coverage globally. It negotiated with Pfizer to cofund development and launch the molecule underlying Lipitor. Warner-Lambert got a $250 million check from Pfizer, thus gaining resources from outside and, at the same time, improving its market position with more sales coverage.

Every year companies such as Colgate-Palmolive and Emerson Electric generate resources that build for the future through productivity-improvement programs. Colgate is one of the very best examples of a company that delivers short-term results quarter after quarter. It has an enviable record of increasing margins every year and outcompeting its major competitors in earnings growth, sales, and cash generation. Not only does its total toothpaste product line make it number one in sales and market share, but its consistent practices every year to develop and execute productivity programs funds the growth projects of the future. Unique among consumer goods companies, Colgate now has a global group working on ideas for growth and productivity.

What Are the Critical Issues Facing the Business?

Every business has half a dozen or so critical issues—the ones that can badly hurt it or prevent it from capitalizing on new opportunities or reaching its objectives. Addressing these usually requires research and thought. Delineating the critical issues in the strategic plan helps focus the preparation and dialogue when it comes time to review the strategy.

LARRY: At Honeywell, in the phone calls I have with managers before a review, I'll ask them what they think the critical issues are. I'll then tell them what *I* think the issues are—not because my views are necessarily different, but because we have to be clear about what the strategic plan needs to address. Later we'll get on the phone again and have an iteration of those four or five issues. Finally I'll say, "Go through your plan, and make sure that we can answer these questions when we have the review."

When it comes time to do the review, we'll start the meeting with the issues we've identified. The managers will give some data, of course—how big the business is, what market share they have, how fast the market is growing, who their competitors are. Then we'll talk about what growth and productivity programs we foresee over the next three years. But the focus is on issues that encumber the business, as well as opportunities that we should spend some time trying to capitalize on.

For example, we identified three critical issues for one of our automotive products in 2002. We weren't doing as well as expected in Japan; how could we improve performance there? What would be the next technological evolution of the product? (It's in a high-tech market that is changing rapidly.) And how could we grow the aftermarket more quickly?

You also have to know what issues to leave out of the discussion. Let's say the question comes up of whether we should build a plant to produce a new product. That question is appropriate for inclusion in the plan, but we shouldn't make a decision without enough detail to really make that judgment as carefully as we can. We may have two or three of these kinds of issues. I want to review the whole plan and then hold a separate session to resolve those big issues.

These "unmentionable" issues are potentially embarrassing to open in front of other people; most involve management failure. The Xerox story discussed in chapter 2 is an example. The highly indebted company's huge consumption of cash and its loss of market share brought it to a financial crisis in the year 2000 because management failed in the execution of its plans to reorganize the sales force by industry and to consolidate its administrative centers. Critical issues such as these need to be the subject of robust dialogue during the building of the plan. If problems arise, they should be placed on the table for discussion by including them in the plan. "Why did we lose market share last year in this business for a key product? Why can't we achieve higher productivity? Why can't we grow more rapidly in China? Why do we continue to have quality problems? How can we continue to grow our market?" You burrow through the five or six issues to provide data and make recommendations and debate, and ultimately you achieve a resolution. That's part of a productive strategic planning exercise.

■ ■ ■

Many strategies fall apart because the right critical issues aren't raised. AT&T's critical issues included the decline in long-distance revenues and the organizational capability to execute a major shift in strategy. The Iridium consortium—the joint effort of Motorola and TRW to develop a satellite telecommunications system able to link phones worldwide—confronted two critical issues. One was how to create enough demand to bring prices down enough to build a sizable market; the other (related to the first) was to develop handheld units small enough that consumers would be able to conveniently carry them around. The strategy failed on both counts.

In 2001 Dell Computer was beginning to face its critical issue—the dim long-term outlook for PCs. No matter how much market share Dell stood to gain, the market had no foreseeable heady growth. An initial step in the right direction was to form an alliance with EMC to market EMC's storage equipment. A stronger option was to expand into the adjacent segment, servers, where the growth potential is far higher than for PCs. But can Dell's low-margin, high-velocity model, which works so well for PCs, be effective with more technologically sophisticated servers? As this book goes to press, the jury is still out.

At the level of the business unit, the issues are smaller in scope but are no less critical to the organization's future. For example, in the Honeywell automotive unit, these were some of the critical issues raised in the 2001 plan.

1. Can we continue to have costs low enough to still make adequate margins in continually declining prices in the automotive segment? What does it take for us to be ahead of the curve on costs?

2. Should the leadership team consider shifting manufacturing to a low-cost location like China? What are the risks in taking such a step?

3. What are the regulatory issues? Are we aware of any negatives, and if so, what are we going to do about them? Are we doing enough to support tighter restrictions on auto emissions, which will increase demand for the product?

How Will the Business Make Money on a Sustainable Basis?

Every strategy must lay out clearly the specifics of the anatomy of the business, how it will make money now and in the future. That means understanding the following foundations, the mix of which is unique for every business: the drivers of cash, margin, velocity, revenue growth, market share, and competitive advantage. For example, the division manager we discussed earlier who was proposing a $300 million investment for a new product would need to present the following information to answer the question about how his strategy for the product would make money and provide adequate return on investment:

- Pricing at different levels of demand. Will the customer pay a premium for what you claim is a differentiation?

- Cost and cost structure now and in the future.

- Cash required for working capital.

- Actions required to ramp up revenue growth.

- The investment required to market the product.

- Continued investments in technologies to prepare for the next generation of product.

- Competitors' pricing reactions.

■ ■ ■

By now we hope you can see that a strategic plan contains ideas that are specific and clear. It is not a numbers exercise. Numbers are obviously needed, but those that are detailed line by line and are mechanically extrapolated over five years offer little in the way of insight. The numbers you need are those that add to the robustness of the ideas in the strategic plan.

The questions are not mechanical, either. The ones that are important will vary from situation to situation and from year to year. So will the answers—what's right for one business today may not be right for another business, or for the same business.

A plan prepared according to the guidelines and questions outlined in this chapter provides the foundation for a robust dialogue linking the strategy to the people and operating processes. That dialogue takes place during the review of strategy detailed in the next chapter.

CHAPTER 8

How to Conduct
a Strategy Review

Maybe you've sat through one or more strategy reviews like this one: The participants gather. The planners bring out the big, fat book they've assembled and go through it page by page in show-and-tell mode, allowing little room for questions. The CEO will ask a few, to be sure. Often he's been prepped by the planning staff so that he can show he has a grasp of the subject (and maybe nail a few people with "gotchas"). People struggle to stay awake through the deadly ritual. At the end of four hours, there's been little or no constructive discussion, and almost no decisions about which actions will advance the business. In fact, nobody really understands much of what they've heard—the critical issues don't stand out amid all the mind-numbing detail. People will take the books back to their offices, where they will end up as credenza-ware, gathering dust for the rest of the year.

This is the business unit strategy review. It's how reviews were conducted at GE before Jack Welch took over more than two decades ago. Others have since adopted the style he brought to GE—ban the fat books, and get everybody thinking and talking about reality. But the message still hasn't really gotten out. Far too many reviews are dominated by dry discussions of numbers and by people maneuvering for power and ducking tough questions.

This is no way to execute. The business unit strategy review is the prime Social Operating Mechanism of the strategy process. It provides the penultimate ground for testing and validating the strategy—the last chance to get things right before the plan faces the ultimate test of the real world. As such, it has to be inclusive and interactive: it must feature a solid debate, conducted in the robust dialogue of the execution culture, with all of the key players present and speaking their minds.

The review should be a creative exercise, not a drill where people regurgitate data. If creativity is absent from the conversation, the participants might as well stay in their offices. People have to leave with closure to the discussion and clear accountability for their parts in the plan, and the leader must follow through to be sure that everyone is clear about the outcome of the review.

LARRY: My son Paul, a vice president for commercial equipment financing at GE Capital, came to me one day. He was going into his first planning session in this new position, and he asked, "Dad, what do you think they're looking for?" I told him, "They're looking for new ideas. Don't go in there and just have a reprise of last year's plan. Make your idea the best idea you can, and don't worry if someone says it's a bad idea. Make it into a creative process where some new thinking happens that wouldn't otherwise have happened. That's an element of a good planning process." While you generally want to avoid the rearview mirror—focusing too much on last year's strategic plan—you should spend some time discussing how well it was executed. How close did you come to achieving its goals? I never ask people for a lot of numbers, just some trend numbers. But then you have to ask, are the trend numbers about the same, and did people do what they said they'd do, or is this just another day in the life of things that don't happen? Search for ways to link as many of these events as possible as a basis for establishing credibility.

■ ■ ■

The strategy review is also a good place for a leader to learn about and develop people. You'll find out about their strategic-thinking capabilities, both as individuals and as a group. At the end of the review, you'll have a good perspective on the people involved and an assessment about their potential for promotion. And you'll have had opportunities to coach people.

QUESTIONS TO RAISE AT A STRATEGY REVIEW

In the strategy review, you'll be going over the same critical issues that you developed in building the strategic plan (chapter 7). But in this expanded group, you'll be getting a fresh diversity of viewpoints. The CFO's staff will be looking at the plan's financial realism. The human resources people will be questioning the implications for leadership development. And so on.

In the end, the discussion must answer the key questions: Is the plan plausible and realistic? Is it internally consistent? Does it match the critical issues and the assumptions? Are people committed to it?

You'll also be raising new questions and sharpening old ones to new levels of specificity. For example:

- How well versed is each business unit team about the competition?

- How strong is the organizational capability to execute the strategy?

- Is the plan scattered or sharply focused?

- Are we choosing the right ideas?

- Are the linkages with people and operations clear?

How Well Versed Is Each Business Unit Team About the Competition?

It goes without saying that the strategy review needs to analyze the competition. Far too often, however, competitor analysis is focused only on past history: industry dynamics, cost structure, market share, brand differentiation, and power in distribution channels. What really counts is not pages of data about what the competition has done in the past, but real-time reporting on what they're up to and likely to do next.

- What are our competitors planning to do to serve their customer segments and prevent us from serving them?

- How good are their sales forces?

- What are our competitors doing to increase market share?

- How will they respond to our product offerings?

- What do we know about the background of our competition's leadership? (If they are from marketing, they may be most likely to respond with new marketing programs; if they are from production, they may try to enhance quality.)

- What do we know about the leader of a fierce competitor and his motivations, and what does that mean for us? (If a competitor has heavy incentives to gain market share, his motivation could well be to prevent us from moving into that segment even if his profitability goes down. He may not sustain falling profitability for long, but will it block our entry.)

- What acquisitions will our key competitors make that will affect us?

- Could a competitor form an alliance and attack our segment? (For example, Sun Microsystems has to carefully evaluate Dell's recent alliance with EMC to accelerate its penetration in the server and storage markets.)

- What new people have competitors added that could alter the competitive landscape? Ford and Chrysler, for example, should be taking a very careful look at what the appointment of Bob Lutz as vice chairman of General Motors signifies. GM has been making steady progress in reducing costs since Rick Wagoner became president and then CEO. Now, by reaching out and bringing in the car world's best product developer, GM has taken a big step in its quest to regain market share. Lutz is not only the flamboyant "car guy" with a great understanding of consumer needs, but a cost-conscious team player. His track record at both Ford and Chrysler in designing and developing new products with shorter development cycles is unparalleled. An effective analysis of the competition at every auto company will demand the team's intellectually honest view of what the addition of Lutz means for each company individually and the industry as a whole.

How Strong Is the Organizational Capability to Execute the Strategy?

Here's where a tight and consistent linkage between strategy and people processes becomes critical. For example, a leading software services company has grown rapidly over the past three years, increasing its contracts from $4 billion in 1999 to $12 billion in 2001. Its sales staff has, for the most part, sold services to the information technology managers of *Fortune* 1000 companies. Its individual contracts with these companies have been in the $500 million range. To maintain its rate of growth, the company now needs to become dominant at *Fortune* 50 companies and increase the size of its contracts to the $2 billion range. Reaching this next level will require selling to CEOs and CFOs, and stressing the dollars-and-cents benefits of the services to the client companies. The new game needs multifunctional teams that can create value propositions that link the services sold with the customer's financial results. This kind of selling can take as long as a year before a contract is closed. And the new team needs to have a better than 50 percent win ratio, up from the previous standard of one in three. Executing the new strategy requires salespeople with the mental capacity to visualize the total needs of the Fortune 50 customer. Questions that need to be asked about organizational capability in situations like this include:

- Do we have the sales force and sales engineers to win in the new market segments, or are they yesterday's people? The answer requires good input from the people process, where the new organizational structure, the leaders' capabilities, and criteria for judging them in the entry phase of this strategy should be discussed in depth.

- Do we know the technology and have a roadmap of how it will change over time?

- Do we have a cost structure that will allow us to compete profitably?

Is the Plan Scattered or Sharply Focused?

As businesses pursue growth by expanding their offerings, they often end up trying to provide more goods and services than they can handle comfortably. General Motors, Procter & Gamble, and many others have fallen victim to this overreaching. After two decades of unfocused growth, Unilever ended up with about 1,600 brands. In 2001 it confronted the problem head on, reducing its brands to some 400. The results have already shown up in higher margins and revenue growth.

Questions to ask:

- Is the plan too ambitious? What are our priorities to avoid fragmentation of effort?

- Is our leadership team taking on too many market segments simultaneously? Will it dilute our focus on our original market segment, to the extent that we could lose the golden goose that is to fund the new segments?

Are We Choosing the Right Ideas?

Many people strategize themselves into the wrong businesses. No matter how well you execute, the risk of failure increases markedly when the ideas you develop don't fit with your existing capabilities, or force you to acquire those capabilities at too high a cost.

For example, a large, $6 billion industrial company with high margins used a network of small distributors to sell its product to customers. In a quest for growth, the company bought many of these distributors in order to build a retail chain. It brought in one of its own executives from Europe to run it, and the entrepreneurs who founded the distributors left. Going into retail was the wrong idea for this company. It had no expertise in retail, didn't understand how to make money in a low-margin business requiring significant logistical expertise, and was not prepared to spend the money necessary to build the capabilities needed to manage a completely different type of business. As a result, the company started to lose money and the stock price went down by a third.

How do you make the right choices? You can get a good idea from how specific, clear, and robust the ideas are. Then you need a lot of dialogue to make sure that even the ideas that sound good make sense. You start by asking four basic questions about each one:

- Is this idea consistent with the realities of the market-place?

- Does it mesh with our organization's capabilities?

- Are we pursuing more ideas than we can handle?

- Will the idea make money?

You get the answers from robust dialogue among the business leaders, with help from the planning staff. Then together you can make a decision about which ideas to pursue.

LARRY: For example, let's assume a business leader wants to enter a new market segment but he doesn't have the right product. You want to know who is in this product segment and what's the growth rate of the segments within it. In addition to evaluating the idea, you've got to visualize how it's going to be adapted in your own environment. You don't want to get into a business where historically you haven't done very well. People do that all the time. Their thinking is, "We haven't been in this business, but we've been in one that looks something like it, and we think we can assimilate the right capabilities to do it." That kind of thinking raises the risk level considerably.

During my AlliedSignal years, someone came to me and said, "We just kind of by accident developed a new flat screen in one of our laboratories, and we want to get into the flat screen business." I looked at the technology, and it seemed to do what they said it would do. I said, "That's wonderful. But we don't have any core technology in manufacturing flat screens. You tell me we can make it, but we don't have any history of making it. We may not even have a culture to deal with it in the right way. Some big players out there have the expertise. How likely is it that we're going to be able to outcompete them over time?" In the end, and after a troublesome start, we licensed the technology to a company that had experience with it.

In other words, you have to not only evaluate the idea but try to anticipate how it's going to fit into your environment. A good idea for a product or service may work at a company like the one that licensed the flat screen but not at a company like AlliedSignal or Honeywell. Good ideas aren't the same for everybody.

Another thing to watch out for is taking on too many projects. Let's say that in the course of reviewing strategic plans for a month across the whole company, four wonderful new ideas surface among the many put forth. In terms of the work that needs to be done, they all will take five to seven years to mature. A lot of people will just go ahead and take on all four ideas. But the programs all throw out big losses to begin with, because that's the nature of things, and then people start to feed them less heartily so that they can reduce the cost of the launches. That extends the time where they can become mature.

When you see four ideas like this, you have to say, "Look, our company isn't big enough to afford all of these. We're going to pick the two best ones and run with them. We can take the losses on them. But we're going to have to make some decisions about the other two. Maybe they'll be gone by the time we get to them, so maybe we should license them now, but we're not going to start four and then starve them and get nothing out of any of them." But in company after company, the appetite is much bigger than the ability to digest, and wrong decisions get made. Too much is taken on that doesn't come to fruition.

The strategy review helps to further articulate the direction of the business. It provides the basis for allocating capital to things that have an attractive future and reducing capital to things that are less attractive.

Are the Linkages with People and Operations Clear?

Achieving everything we've talked about so far depends on linking the strategy process to the people and operations processes well. The more you and your people know about all three, the better judgments and trade-offs you can make about how well your strategy meshes with your capabilities, and whether it has a reasonable chance of being profitable.

The linkage between strategy and operations becomes totally transparent when the first few pages of the operating plan (see chapter 9) describe the new strategic direction, the resources required, and the programs to be executed quarter by quarter in the next year.

The auto manufacturer supplier we discussed in chapter 7 had executed a strategy that moved it from a breakeven commodity business to the supplier of choice by the top ten industrial customers around the world. It now wants to move to the next level by servicing new customers in adjacent segments. In the strategy review the

217

kind of questions about linkage to people and operations should include:

The strategy of a business unit clearly lays out how it will reach a new set of customers and ways to get the product qualified in the new segment.

- If a new organizational structure is required, what new sales management skills will be needed?

- Are financial resources assigned in the next year's budget to build whatever is required to launch entry into the new segment?

- What are the programs for each quarter? How will the programs be funded quarter by quarter? Will the need for quarterly profits squeeze out these programs? (Superior leaders make the right trade-offs between the short and long terms.)

Or suppose you want to go to the next level by moving into an adjacent segment? How do you get into the potential customers' doors? And how do you get their people to qualify the new product—that is, make sure it meets their specifications and needs? Each of these is both a people and an operations issue, raising such questions as:

- Do you have the right kinds and numbers of people to do these things?

- Have you allotted enough lead time for the required actions?

LARRY: A good strategic plan has to be translatable

into the operating plan. Not all in one year, but it has to have an action quotient to it. Sometimes you go into these two processes, and they make you think you're in two different companies. You review the strategic plan, and you don't recognize any aspect of it when you review the operating plan—and vice versa.

For an operating review, I like to quickly review the strategic plan to see that link has been established. I want the first three pages of the document to be a summary of the strategic plan. The agreed-upon components of the strategic plan must have a seamless transition into the operating plan. Suppose in the strategic plan we determine that we are going to spend money to launch a new product that will complement our existing products, and we determine what its costs will be, the level of success we expect it to have, and that it will be tested with customers. In the operating plan, we need to make sure that it has an R&D plan of action that is funded at a level to carry out the strategic goal.

Do your strategic assumptions mesh with your internal yardsticks? You have to define what you do and don't want to invest in, and the strategy compilations have to agree with those judgments. Internal indicators would include businesses you want to be in, businesses you don't want to be in, businesses you want to invest in, and businesses you want to harvest.

Suppose somebody comes to you with a plan for growing his business's revenues at 15 percent a year. He's a good leader, one who always makes his commitments. But you've noted that his market segment is growing at only 3 percent a year. How is he going to achieve 15 percent growth—and at what cost? Is achieving a bigger share of this slow-growth market worth the investment you'll have to make—in product development, marketing, acquisitions, or whatever it is that will supposedly drive this growth? Maybe you can put the capital to better use.

Or suppose somebody comes to you and says the business should go ahead and pursue those four good ideas I mentioned earlier. Looking at the other parts of the business gives me enough data to ask, "How much capital are you going to put into these four new ideas, and what are their operating losses?" If she can't give me good answers, I may have to say. "Look, we can't afford to do all four of these. You pick out two, and we'll fund them and then see if we can get to the other two depending on" whatever. I don't want to finish reading the strategic plan, which calls for developing all four ideas, and then turn to the operating plan and have to say, "Oh, my God, look at this. We can't do all four of these." She would say, "Well, we had all the ideas in the strategic plan, and you said you liked them. We put them in the operating plan. Now you come and you throw them out."

When a business decides on a new strategy, it needs to have a dialogue about the quality and aptitude of the people involved. At Honeywell we decided to get into the electronic packaging business, that is, designing and developing chips for electronic motherboards. But we did not have people with the right technical background and manufacturing expertise. We got into the business and lost money, but we never had to demonstrate that we had the right capabilities. We had had an effective dialogue that recognized our capability shortfall, but we'd decided that we could overcome it. It turned out we couldn't. The person who had proposed the program had been very persuasive, and we hadn't had the courage to say no. We bet on the man and the organization, and in neither case was it enough to make shareholders happy.

■ ■ ■

Throughout the processes outlined above, asking questions constantly keeps the critical issues in mind: Do you have the right leaders in the right jobs? How well do they work together? Do you have enough of the kind of people you need? Do you have the production, financial, and technological resources to execute the strategy?

FOLLOWING THROUGH

At the end of the strategy review, write a letter to each of the leaders to solidify and confirm the agreements you made so that later you can use them as the basis for reviewing progress. The letter should talk about growth and new products, and it should establish the link between strategy and people and operations. The following letter is typical of the letters that business unit leaders got at AlliedSignal and that they get today at Honeywell:

Date: June 22, XXXX
To: Jane Smith
From: Larry Bossidy
Subject: X Systems Strategic Plan Review

This is a great business and a nice plan. Here are some specific comments.

• We must recognize that we are a target for our competitors. You should think about how we might attack ourselves if we were the competition. These are very

221

competent companies, and we cannot become complacent. Remember, most firms whose substantial market position gets eroded are beaten either on cost or on technology. We must be prepared to compete on both.

- We should defend our current position in Europe. This region still appears to provide plenty of growth potential, and we do not want to create easy opportunities for competitors to gain a foothold here.
- We must identify the goals and vision of our customers. This will make it easier for us to plan for the future and will improve our ability to anticipate and meet customers' needs.
- Licensing our brands could be a nice program. We need to be careful how and where this is done, to avoid adverse affects on our business.
- The relationship with customer A and the recovery at customer B are terrific. The B situation in southern Europe was a big wake-up call, and it appears that you have responded well. Now we need to become more consistent in our customer service, especially if we expect to maintain a premium price.
- We obviously cannot fund all of the projects in this plan. You have to prioritize your opportunities and, for those further down the list, look for creative funding such as government programs.
- The wheel portfolio chart is a nice way to view our position. You should use it to track our progress.
- You should have a very receptive customer base for product Y. Customers D, E, and F all need to find ways to improve their performance in this segment, and this is one product that can help them.
- As we implement our aftermarket strategy, we must make sure that we are still meeting our customer

needs. The small remanufacturing shops must deliver at least the level of service we currently provide.

- The K group has done a nice job, although it is not clear that we can sustain our edge here.
- The Z business is on target. We must watch for new competition and keep an eye on our costs.
- We need a detailed and well-thought-out plan for our plants, one that considers the ZZ program as well as the current products. It is important to get this right the first time.
- We need distribution partners that add value for ZZ. We do not need brokers for our product.
- It is important to keep an eye on our competitors' systems capabilities and find the right partner to develop our own.
- You must continue to involve our lobbyist group to show congressional leaders the advantages of the product and dispel some of the current misconceptions.
- We need to improve our manufacturing capability before we offer new products. Although we have made improvements, our spare parts delivery rates are still unacceptable.
- We need to make Six Sigma translate into higher productivity. In the end, we are competing on cost, quality, and technology. We have to be in a position to win on cost. We should develop a progressive manufacturing strategy to keep our costs low.
- As we add to our current capacity, we should think about flexible capacity. We should be prepared for the eventual downturn in this market. Thailand makes sense, but I'm not sure about the Midwest.
- Before we establish sourcing and manufacturing in Asia, we should understand the effects of changes in the currency rates. We need to decide whether it would

still make sense if the Asian currencies were to appreciate. We also must determine which components can be sourced locally and which can't. We must be confident that our core suppliers can meet our needs, both in quantity and quality. This is particularly important as we make our decision on location X.

- The BBB program is impressive. It should greatly improve our cycle time and engineering efficiency. The standard parts library will be a big opportunity for us.
- We have to be aggressive in patenting and defending our intellectual property. Look at competitor X closely to see if they are infringing on our patents.
- The CCC opportunity is nice, but still a ways away. Competitor Y has as much technology as anyone in this market. You should look to them for ideas.
- As we move to DDD technology, we should try to make it as simple as possible. We can still capture the majority of the value without adding all the potential complexity of these programs.
- Keep training high on the priority list; make it as broad as you can.
- We must develop a diverse leadership team to match the global needs of this business.
- This is a good plan that will require a lot of work and leadership. This is a wonderful business with many opportunities. You need to set priorities for your growth projects to get the maximum returns on our investment. Finally, be sure to communicate your strategic thinking and programs to your entire organization. Their commitment and involvement will drive your success.

■ ■ ■

In these chapters on strategy and earlier in our discussion of the people process, we have laid out processes to determine where the leadership wants to take the business and who is going to get it there. We now move to the specifics on a short-term time scale of four quarters. The outcome of this process, which we call operations, is a commitment. This process is where the moving parts in an organization are aligned.

CHAPTER 9

The Operations Process: Making the Link with Strategy and People

Your boss has asked you to drive from Chicago to Oskaloosa, Iowa, a journey of 317 miles. He's prepared a budget for you with clear metrics. You can spend no more than $16 on gas, you must arrive in 5 hours and 37 minutes, and you can't drive over 60 miles per hour. But no one has a map with a route to Oskaloosa, and you don't know whether you'll run into a snowstorm on the way.

Ludicrous? No more so than the way many companies translate their strategic plans into operations. They do it through a budgeting process that spells out the results you're supposed to achieve, such as revenues, cash flow, and earnings, and the resources you're allotted to achieve them. But the process doesn't deal with how—or even whether—you can get the results, so it is disconnected from reality. What you need is what you find in companies that execute: a robust operating process, centered on an operating plan that links strategy and people to results.

The strategy process defines where a business wants to go, and the people process defines who's going to get it there. The operating plan provides the path for those people. It breaks long-term output into short-term targets. Meeting those here-and-now targets forces decisions to be made and integrated across the organization, both initially and in response to changes in business conditions. It puts reality behind the numbers. The operating plan is not budgeting for "We did better than last year." Such budgeting looks into the rearview mirror to set its goals; an operating plan looks forward to the *hows*.

An operating plan includes the programs your business is going to complete within one year to reach the desired levels of such objectives as earnings, sales, margins, and cash flow. Among these programs are product launches; the marketing plan; a sales plan that takes advantage of market opportunities; a manufacturing plan that stipulates production outputs; and a productivity plan that improves efficiency. The assumptions on which the operating plan is based are linked to reality and are debated among the finance people and the line leaders who have to execute. For example, what effects will the growth or decline of the GDP and the level of interest rates and inflation have on the specific businesses covered by the plan? What happens if an important customer changes his plans in a big way? The operating plan specifies how the various moving parts of the business will be synchronized to achieve the targets, deals with trade-offs that need to be made, and looks at contingencies for the things that can go wrong or offer unexpected opportunities.

We've made the point repeatedly that leaders have to be intimately involved in the three core processes and know the business—which they get in good measure from just that involvement. In the operating plan, the leader is primarily responsible for overseeing the seamless transition

227

from strategy to operations. She has to set the goals, link the details of the operations process to the people and strategy processes, and lead the operating reviews that bring people together around the operating plan. She has to make timely, incisive judgments and trade-offs in the face of myriad possibilities and uncertainties. She has to conduct robust dialogue that surfaces truth. And she must, all the while, be teaching her people how to do these things as well. At the same time, the leader is learning—about her people, and how they behave when the rubber meets the road, and about the pitfalls that beset elegant strategies.

It's not just the leader alone who has to be present and involved. All of the people accountable for executing the plan need to help construct it.

LARRY: An operating plan is not about green eye-shades putting numbers together. It's a total responsibility. It ties a thread through people, strategy, and operations, and it translates into assigning goals and objectives for the next year.

You really want the operating plan to be owned by everybody. The more people you get involved in the plan, either through contingency plans or projects that have to be undertaken in the coming year—the more people who are aware of the expectations for them—the more you achieve.

■ ■ ■

Such an operations process couldn't be more different from the typical budget struggle. We see three major flaws in the budgeting or operations process at most companies. First, the process doesn't provide for robust dialogue on the plan's assumptions. Second, the budget is built around the results that top management wants, but it doesn't discuss or specify the action programs that will make those outcomes a reality. Third, the process doesn't provide coaching opportunities for people to learn the totality of the business, or develop the social architecture of working together in common cause.

These operating plans are typically based on a budget that has been previously prepared. This is backward: the budget should be the financial expression of the operating plan and the underlying plans generated by the business's components, rather than the other way around.

Budgets often have little to do with the reality of execution because they're numbers and gaming exercises, where people spend months figuring out how to protect their interests instead of focusing on the business's critical issues. The financial targets are often no more than the increases from the previous year's results that top management thinks security analysts expect. Down at the lower levels, people put out minimum bids for what they can do to beat those results. Often they'll sandbag, proposing numbers lower than those they think they can achieve. Then they'll negotiate with their bosses. Maybe they'll come up and the bosses will come down. Or maybe the bosses will say, "No, these are our targets, and you will meet them." No one necessarily knows how and why those numbers are reached, but they nonetheless become marching orders for the coming fiscal year.

The process drains energy, diverting it into useless game playing. And the resulting rigid budget can lead to missed opportunities over the course of the year. Let's say that during the second quarter you've come up with a workable plan that could raise the market share of your business by two points before the year's end. Fulfilling the plan would take a small investment, but the likelihood of success is so great that it could put you over the top in terms of market share, and the payback will be less than one year. You present the plan to your boss and sit silently while he reads it. Finally he looks at you sadly and says, "It's a great proposal, Bob. But there's no money in the budget for it."

Such a budget can also force people to make poor decisions when they're desperate to reach their targets. One common practice, for example, is loading inventory into the pipeline just before the end of a quarter—often on overtime—to pump up the numbers. But the business will have to pay a price next quarter, when the managers will have to discount sharply or compromise manufacturing efficiency by cutting back production.

RAM: Most companies build their budgets or operating plans with a system designed by accounting people. The leaders set the goals using hortatory slogans like "fifteen-five": 15 percent growth per annum over the next five years. Everybody goes around parroting it. The leaders say that half the growth will come "organically," meaning from business that the organization already has, and half will come from acquisition. These aspirations show the leaders to be visionary. The CFO calculates that margins will improve, debt will be lowered, and the stock price will quadruple. But ask these leaders how they're going to achieve these goals, and what assumptions the goals are based on, and they'll have no idea. "We're going to work on that," they explain. Then each business unit does its planning compared with last year and unconnected to the overall picture, with no common understanding or connection and no simultaneous dialogue.

This kind of budget process defeats the very purpose of planning. In the months between the time the budget preparations begin and final approval (some take as long as four months), the environment has probably changed. But the assumptions behind the budget remain. A static document in an active world, it reduces the organization's flexibility to respond to change. And it does nothing to help people synchronize the many moving parts of the organization.

One CEO is wrestling with this problem now. His company has five businesses, and the stock price has been static for the past five years. Two years ago he came from another company, and he's done a good job of improving productivity, but growth has been much less than the aspirations. Unless its performance improves and the stock market rewards it with higher price/earnings ratios, the company will have difficulty making many big acquisitions.

The CEO has laid out a five-year aspiration to inspire people to see what is possible. To flesh out his strategic plan, he's gotten his top hundred people together for two days to elicit ideas and get them fired up. He's now gotten each of his business units to think about new ways to create growth: new value propositions, new channels, new customers. He is changing beliefs, behaviors, people, and resource allocation. He's integrating horizontally by getting business units to sell together in the same channels. Now he's creating an operating plan that has quarter-by-quarter action steps.

HOW TO BUILD A BUDGET IN THREE DAYS

Most sizable businesses spend weeks or months preparing their budgets. This is unnecessary, and a great waste of time. You probably recognize that it can and should be done much faster. But would you believe you can prepare your budget in three days? We know a number of companies that do it.

The starting point is a robust dialogue among all the relevant business leaders, who sit down together to understand the whole corporate picture, including all of the relationships among its parts. We call this the principle of simultaneity.

Almost all budget or operating plan exercises are done sequentially, bottom up and top down: the goals and general assumptions come from the top, and the businesses generate the particulars. But sequential budgeting misses the power of simultaneous dialogue, which generates insights on the totality of the business and links its moving parts into a whole.

The dialogue takes place in a three-day session that includes all of the business unit leader's direct reports, line and staff. They've all previously been given the initial cut at the broad assumptions for the external environment, along with a set of competitor analyses and the financial and other targets for the year, quarter by quarter.

The meeting focuses on the roughly twenty lines that, in just about any budget, account for 80 percent of the impact on the business outcomes. Among these, for example, are revenues by product mix, operating margins, marketing expenses, manufacturing costs, engineering and development expenses, and so forth. The leader starts by having each function present its action plans for meeting the proposed budget. He questions the assumptions to test their validity and asks how each action plan will affect the other businesses. For example, if a manager wants to cut her price to generate more volume, that will raise a yellow flag for manufacturing: What will the added costs be? Will it entail overtime? Other functions raise further questions.

After everyone's had his or her say, the group breaks up for an hour, and each manager discusses the information with his subteam. The manufacturing people, for example, will figure out how much they can cut costs given the higher volume and therefore how much room there is to reduce prices. They'll talk about alternatives: Should they add a third shift, or outsource? Where will they secure more components?

When the groups reconvene, they all load their information into a common computer spreadsheet program. Within moments they have a picture of what this budget would look like. They can see in real time what makes sense and what doesn't, and how well all of the components synchronize. Then they'll go through the process again, questioning, reshaping, and refining. Usually they're finished after four cycles. They've got their basic budget and operating plans; they'll fill the rest of the budget lines and flesh out the plans after they return to their offices.

Don't bother to try this if you can't handle dialogue that reveals conflict or negotiate trade-offs persuasively— or if you're the kind of insecure individual who gets his power from hoarding information. But if you're up for it, this process will give you a reality-based budget that you can follow with confidence and adapt to changes in the business environment as they arise. Everyone will understand how they fit into the overall business. You'll find that people will be able to move faster and will be more willing to experiment with good ideas, knowing they aren't trapped in a rigid and probably obsolete budget structure.

You'll also find it's a powerful team-building exercise.

THE IMPORTANCE OF SYNCHRONIZATION

Synchronization is essential for excellence in execution and for energizing the corporation. Synchronization means that all the moving parts of the organization have common assumptions about the external environment over the operating year and a common understanding— the left hand knows what the right hand is doing. Synchronizing includes matching the goals of the interdependent parts and linking their priorities with other parts of the organization. When conditions change, synchronization realigns the multiple priorities and reallocates resources.

For example, take an automobile company with ten brands and some three million combinations of options and colors, more than a hundred plants around the globe, hundreds of suppliers, thousands of dealers, and half a dozen ad agencies. Each of these components makes decisions every day, and they are in motion, always changing. When interest rates go down, not all market segments grow equally, not all brands are required to expand output equally, and not all dealers will sell equally more cars. So they have to be synchronized to take advantage of the differential market segments by geography, dealer, and the like.

In a large company it's a complex task. For example, when somebody decides to promote a new item, they need six months' lead time to order it. The moving parts are advertising, promotion, stocking the shelves, and logistics (which is often outsourced). If something outside changes, the relationships have to change. For example, if demand declines, the relationships among advertising, promotion, planning for production, and inventory levels have to change. But change how? What becomes more important and less important? Operating systems in companies that execute well, such as GE, Wal-Mart, Dell, and Colgate-Palmolive, synchronize these things faster and better than others.

September 11 created real concern in Detroit that demand for vehicles would tank. And it did indeed disappear for a few days. Ron Zarella, General Motors' vice president for North America, conceived of zero percent financing, and implementing it put demand in high gear. Never was there a better time for it. In November, the Federal Reserve continued to reduce interest rates, to a forty-year low of 1.75 percent. Consumers were able to refinance and gain cash for down payments. Demand shot from a rate of 16 million units annually to 21 million plus.

The move required an operating plan to reprogram and reallocate resources and to synchronize GM's various moving parts. How many of which kinds of vehicles should GM build? In which plants? Which regions would require what mix of products? How much advertising money should the company spend, and where, and on which products? If production and advertising did not balance, the result would be a double negative: With margins cut by the zero percent financing, an imbalance between production and advertising would both lose sales and raise costs.

This program opened up a big opportunity for GM. Though other automakers joined quickly, GM's swift execution gave the company an immediate boost in market share. And GM went all out with it because it felt the program could be not just a one-shot measure but a chance to reverse its three-decade decline in market share. Cost cutting had begun to improve the company's productivity. Vice chairman Bob Lutz, the celebrated "car guy" who led Chrysler's hot product streak, was already making decisions that would show up in the current year's advertising and in next year's vehicles. GM's premise was that the marketplace momentum and higher morale generated by the program would help it hang on to the gains and even increase them.

SOUND ASSUMPTIONS: THE KEY TO SETTING REALISTIC GOALS

An operating plan addresses the critical issues in execution by building the budget on realities. What do the capital markets expect, and what are your assumptions about the business environment? If it's sunshine, how do you take advantage of the opportunities better than your competitors? If it's rain, what actions do you need to perform to ride out the storm better than them?

How well do your business leaders understand this, and how imaginative are they in capitalizing on the changes? How good are they at robust dialogue, with which they can grasp reality and act without needing to wait for the approval of higher-level people?

■ ■ ■

Debate on assumptions is one of the most critical parts of any operating review—not just the big-picture assumptions but assumptions specifically linked with their effects on the business, segment by segment, item by item. That's a key part of what's missing in the standard budget review. You cannot set realistic goals until you've debated the assumptions behind them.

In budget and operating plan negotiations, there's an inherent conflict of interests. People bring assumptions to the negotiations through the lenses of their functions and their positions. For example, a production man wants to have the lowest possible costs, so he wants to build the maximum amount of product and have a stable production level. The sales leader likes the idea of having lots of product too; the more she has on the shelf, the better chance she has of making a sale. And why shouldn't they press for their assumptions? Both of their incentives are linked to their specific functional achievements.

The finance officer, on the other hand, is saying, "Wait a minute, I don't see this kind of growth in the economy. We'll wind up with a ton of inventory, which will cut into our cash. Then we'll have to discount it and spend a lot of extra promotion money to get rid of it."

In the standard budget review, they'll all negotiate from their assumptions and reach some sort of compromise. But what you really want to do is get all of the assumptions out in the open, with everyone present and a leader who asks penetrating questions. Then you want to test those assumptions, by going to customers or some other source, to be sure they're valid. With this kind of information, the group can make intelligent trade-offs based on reality. That's what you do in an operating review.

Debating the assumptions and making trade-offs openly in a group is an important part of the social software. It builds the business leadership capacities of all the people involved. As they construct and share a common comprehensive picture of what's happening on the outside and the inside, they hone their ability to synchronize efforts for execution. And they publicly make their commitments to execute.

LARRY: You have to debate the underlying assumptions before you even begin to think about a financial expression of numbers. As a leader, you question all the way down the line whether people have thought through all the ingredients in the plan. You need to be able to identify any assumptions that might be troublesome, in case they don't spot them. You are not saying in the back of your mind, There's no way these guys are going to make this plan, so as to later smile and say, "I told you so." You want to do all you can to help them make the plan.

For example, if I saw a big fourth-quarter sales spike in somebody's plan, I'd say, "Why? What's going to happen in the fourth quarter that's going to cause this? I don't want you to go into the plan with an unrealistic challenge. I want it to be ambitious. I want it to be a little bit of a stretch, but I want it to be achievable."

You need a range of assumptions—some negative, and a couple positive. For example, suppose you've got labor negotiations coming up in your business. If they go badly, you may need a plan to build inventories in case of a strike. Or what do you do if your research budget, for reasons that you can't anticipate now, overruns by $5 million? From what other parts of the business are you going to get the $5 million? Or, on the upside, what will happen if your sales double? How do you get your manufacturing organization aligned so that it can produce that kind of volume? What do you do if you run into shortages of parts that require long lead times?

You don't want to hold these debates too soon, by the way. It's important to make an operating plan as timely as you can. People often put numbers together way too early. I like to see the thinking start in August but not the detailed numbers. Start with some ideas about what the sales and earnings of each component will be (you can't develop the ideas and the numbers independently of each other), but keep in mind that these numbers will be at ten thousand feet. The plan shouldn't get granulated—exposed in detail—until all the thinking about the components is completed. We finalize our plan in November.

■ ■ ■

What kinds of assumptions are we talking about? They cover the lot—anything that can affect your business requires some kind of assumption.

First and foremost: Who is the customer? How does he buy it, and why? What's the need? How long will the need last? What is the competition doing? Is your value proposition good enough?

And if you're an industrial business: Who is the customer's customer? Or even the customer's *customer's* customer? His demands or problems are going to affect your customer. Many people look myopically at their primary customers and don't pay enough attention to the customers who ultimately determine demand for their products.

RAM: After the telecommunications bubble burst, Cisco Systems was slow to face reality. When the company finally changed course, most of its suppliers were stuck with the huge amounts of inventory that they'd been building based on the company's unwarranted optimism. Not so a small Portland, Oregon, supplier. Well before Cisco finally announced its cutbacks, this CEO had asked his board members what they knew about the capital expansion plans of such Cisco customers as Verizon, AT&T, and British Telecom. He also watched the behavior of those companies' biggest customers, such as GM and American Express. As a result of the information he gathered, he came to the conclusion that Cisco's optimism was misguided. He temporarily closed one of his plants in advance and was able to preserve his liquidity.

■ ■ ■

How will your competitors react to your moves? Will they change their pricing? What do you know about their coming product introductions? Will one of them launch a marketing campaign to muscle deeper into your territory?

Your suppliers: Will they be able to deliver enough, just in time, at the right prices? If they're in other countries, what will currency fluctuations do to your costs?

Your distribution channels: Are they delivering on time and billing accurately? Are they financially sound, or will you have to extend credit? Do you have the best ones, or are new ones overtaking them—on the Internet, for example? What will you do if a competitor comes into a distributor you use with greater volume, putting you at a disadvantage?

The economy: What's the outlook not just in the aggregate but for the various market segments and regions you serve?

After September 11, 2001, companies everywhere rushed to redo budgets and strategic plans. The top management team at Honeywell revised its operating plan, as Larry discusses next. Some of the responses may be predictable, but notice the things debated that would have been easy to overlook in the traditional budget and planning processes of a nonexecution company.

LARRY: We had a preliminary 2002 operating plan under construction and had gone over some assumptions. We saw the aerospace industry beginning to soften even before the events of September 11, so we had tried to take that into account by trimming our workforce.

With the events of September 11, a lot of good work went out the window. The airline industry was suddenly in a crisis, with losses projected at $4 billion in the fourth quarter alone. There was concern about whether they could be solvent, given the need to refund enormous numbers of tickets for people who'd elected not to fly. On the other hand, the government had shown at least some interest in providing a form of subsidy, the exact amount and time of which was yet to be known. At the same time, the airlines said they would probably fly something like 80 percent of their regularly scheduled flights in 2002. The spare parts business, the most profitable part of our aerospace business, stopped almost immediately because the airlines ceased ordering when they shut down for several days.

The question before us was how to arrive at a realistic assessment both for the fourth quarter and for the year 2002. We gathered a lot of information, had a number of phone calls, and finally concluded that we probably would lose sales in the range of $1.2 billion—a lot of it in our high-margin aftermarket segment. The defense sales would probably not pick up until later in 2002, because there's always a timing difference between the mobilization of forces and the actual material procurement.

We thought the business aviation segment—corporate jets—would get better sometime next in the coming year, once restrictions on where they could fly were resolved. Because the inconvenience of flying on commercial jets would increase, we concluded that more people would buy either their own planes or so-called fractionals—fractional ownership of business jets, like condo time-sharing. So we had a lesser reduction in the aftermarket for our business and aviation segments, which are both about the same size.

Factoring in those considerations, we said earnings would be down roughly in the range of $500 million from lower operating margins. Then we had to ask how we would get $500 million of cost out of the business. Aspiring for growth in this environment would not have been realistic, so we set our target at staying level in earnings with 2000.

I got a detailed plan from the businesses as to what they were going to do on the cost side to deal with this decline in sales and ultimately operating margin. Once we reached agreement on that, we spread it out among four quarters. A lot of people at the time were arguing that while the fourth quarter, the first quarter, and perhaps even part of the second would be worse because of September 11, the second half would likely be better—the recovery might accelerate after the economy dipped more than we'd originally anticipated before September 11. But we did not build that into our forecast. If that were to be the case, we'd have to mobilize faster. We might lose some sales on the upside. Nonetheless, that's a better risk to take than trying to anticipate a recovery that gets delayed.

At the same time, the airlines were asking for extended terms on their financial obligations, and we had to be responsive to these requests. So we asked for extended terms from our supply base—we don't want to be the financer of last resort.

Most of the other businesses were going to be hurt by a general softening of the economy, so we went through the same drill. What were the sales likely to be? What would be the margin loss? Some businesses had profit growth objectives, so what expenses would they have to take out? What programs would we employ to drive sales staffs during the slowdown? What would be the productivity programs? What about the digitization programs

242

that could help us get productivity growth consistent with what we needed to achieve our objective?

On the other hand, we had some areas that looked promising despite the overall economy. I'll talk about one in detail, here and in the sections that follow. This was an automotive product with growth potential globally.

In preparing our economic assumptions for this automotive product, we looked at four areas. First, we looked at the legislative situation, since the product has to do with emissions control in each major market. Where were regulations going to be tightened? Second, we looked at the macroeconomic environment or worldwide GDP growth. Third, we looked at the underlying environment for motor vehicles specifically in each geographical area.

Fourth, we analyzed each major automotive market in the world—Europe, the Americas, and Asia—since each has different needs. Our product also affects fuel efficiency, so we looked at the requirements for that in each country of the major markets. While I won't go into the myriad details behind each of these assumptions, taken as a whole they played a big role in assessing the product's potential.

For example, the combination of fast economic growth in China, toughening emission standards, and the continuing growth in demand for small vehicles made the Asian market one with very high potential. The European market has good economic fundamentals, but our served market segment is flat.

Though another market segment in North America will contract by 14 percent, penetration in the Americas is low, and the expanding use in some subsets of the segment is favorable for the product. We could also see profitable growth from introducing a new technology.

We also took a careful look at the growing consolidation among our commercial vehicle customers. For each major customer, we projected revenues for 2001 and paid special attention to key developments that would affect them. We foresaw greater competition from two key competitors for the business of one key customer, and we analyzed the capacity for growth, product program launches, and the likelihood of strong or weak interest in our product across the entire customer base.

BUILDING THE OPERATING PLAN

Once the assumptions are pinned down, the next step in the operations process is to build the operating plan itself, which takes place in the operating review. It's a three-part process that begins with setting the targets. In the second part, you develop the action plans, including making the necessary trade-offs between short-term objectives and long-term goals. You also try to identify areas where people can develop contingency plans. Finally, you get agreement and closure from all the participants, establishing follow-through measures to make sure people are meeting their commitments or to work up corrective steps if they aren't.

The operating plan starts by identifying the key targets: revenues, operating margin, cash flow, productivity, market share, and so forth (see Figure 3). The particulars will vary from business to business, but what's important is that they give a one-page overview focused on the things that will drive the improvement in results. These are set from the outside in and from the top down. Outside in means these numbers have to reflect both the economic and competitive environment, and what investors need to see in order to satisfy themselves that the stock is more worth owning than that of your peers. Top down means that the targets are also set from the whole to the part— that is, for the business as a whole, with subsets for its various components. Too many companies do it the other way around, using the budgeting process to get plans

FIGURE 3: SUMMARY FINANCIALS			
	2002	**2003**	**2004**
Revenues			
SG&A (% of sales)			
RD&E (% of sales)			
Operating margin (income)			
Cash flow			
Productivity			
Capital Expenditure			
ROI			

Census
    Salary
    Hourly			

This one-page financial overview includes pieces of information not usually included in the operations review: productivity, a census of employees, the investments this year that will show up in future years.

from the various levels of each business and then assembling them into a whole. This creates a lot of wasted effort, since the numbers have to be redone again and again as people negotiate them.

Usually the final financial target is earnings per share. It depends heavily on the targets for revenues, the foundation on which the action plans are built. People make a huge mistake when they automatically increase some number over last year without discussing the challenges of meeting higher revenue targets and eliciting creative ideas. Such robust discussions should address things like pricing, the mix of customers, the mix of products and channels, advertising and promotion, the quality, quantity, and turnover of the sales staff, and assumptions about the economy, competition, and competitive reactions.

Most important, the discussions must include close attention to gross margins. Too many people look for revenue gains without planning to build or protect gross margins at the same time. But gross margins are where the bottom line comes from—all operating expenses are deducted from the gross margin, not the revenues. Everything flows from gross margins. If you can't get the pricing you need to achieve them, then you have to cut costs.

RAM: A $10 billion industrial company, one of the top in its global industry, was hit hard by recession even before September 11, as well as by the entry of a new competitor from Asia. The company anticipated that revenues in 2002 would shrink by about $1 billion, and the CEO constructed his operating plan around that assumption. But he didn't focus on gross margins. One of his confidants looked at his projections and pointed out that margins would suffer considerably more than revenues, declining from 25 to 20 percent because of the industry's deflationary environment. The friend advised him to redo his plan to meet the shortfall: put variable cost productivity improvement in high gear, cut his headquarters staff in half, and take a management layer out. He took the point, and within a week he had a plan geared to the fundamental desired level of gross margin operating margin.

■ ■ ■

The operating plan covers all the major programs for the coming year—marketing and sales, production, functional operations, capital spending, and so on. In a multi–business unit corporation, these plans originate with the business units as responses to the challenges posed by the targets. We saw something of how such a plan is built in the account of Honeywell's response to the crisis of September 11. Here's how it developed for the specific automotive product.

LARRY: For the plan that the product's business unit manager prepared, the assumptions we agreed on showed revenue growth in the high teens for the South American and Asian markets. The plan then projected revenue and operating margins for each region, and the key initiatives that would support such growth. For example, in the Asian market we planned to support customers in dealing with that region's growing environmental concern. We also had a program to develop new customers in China and to promote sales of high tech globally, using China as a low-cost supply base.

Another program involved the independent aftermarket—manufacturers who supply replacement equipment—which we analyzed as a profitable segment with significant growth opportunity. The initiative centered on the following key issues:

- Fixing delivery and improving product availability.

- Implementing weekly performance reviews to drive tactical action planning.

- Implementing lead times with customers' and distributors' stocking strategies.

We determined revenues by analyzing the mix of products and customers, segment by segment and region by region. In constructing the target for revenues and operating margins for each of these segments, we determined which factors or assumptions would either increase or decrease demand. At the same time, we wanted to know whether we could increase prices or whether pricing would face downward pressure. The answer to these questions varied among the segments and regions according to the different competitive dynamics and health of the customers' industries.

Several other factors can affect revenues. For example, in determining the target for one Honeywell division for 2001, the factors included new applications in one product segment and an acquisition in another segment. This total growth would be offset by flat demand in another segment, particularly in North America. But overall market conditions meant that we expected net significant growth. Foreign exchange and pricing considerations also influenced the final number.

In setting targets for operating margins, we paid special attention to key initiatives, such as new and highly differentiated product offerings, that can command better prices and margins.

THE ART OF MAKING TRADE-OFFS

As they translate strategies into action, operating plans come up against the kind of trade-off issues we noted in chapters 7 and 8. Some strategies contain very specific and clear ideas that will grow the business profitably but that require investment in the current operating period. In such cases the leadership has to make trade-offs.

Where the business makes this investment (whether in technology, products, customer segments, or geographic regions) is deduced from and directly linked to the strategy dialogue. In operations, the leader then ensures as follow-through that strategy direction is specific and clear and still relevant; that it is translated into action by allocating resources; and that the sources of those resources are explicit. She also ensures that accountability is assigned and followed through in subsequent reviews.

If your business has to cut expenses during the operating period, the manager cannot cut this investment unilaterally. The decision has to be made in a debate that includes the CEO, who is the link with the strategic plan. Which product lines do you fund, and which not? Or can you apply some creativity to finding resources that will let you build the business for the future? Perhaps you can get more high-margin products into the mix, or put on an intense sales drive to generate incremental volumes. Or maybe you wanted to shut down a plant this year and transfer production to a lower-cost country. Should you postpone the move by a year, which would avoid the attendant short-term costs, including severance pay? In a consumer goods company, should you take the risk of increasing advertising expenditures in hopes of generating volume? If so, do you advertise more or use more couponing?

The dialogue will also focus on the quality of the people who will make this investment successful. Again, the CEO must be part of it—she is the link with the people process.

An enduring wellspring of resources is the constant drive to increase productivity. Companies like GE, Emerson Electric, and Colgate-Palmolive, which have shown consecutive earnings-per-share increases for fifteen or more years, excel at investing money in the short run for future growth because they get disciplined year by year by productivity improvements. In one year a $1 billion Honeywell division got $30 million from reducing general and administrative expenses. It used that money, along with $7 million it got from improving product mix, to invest in developing new products. Over time this kind of attention to productivity is building a cumulative competitive advantage for the division. Thus $37 million for product development in a $1 billion division gives it a huge competitive advantage.

Some trade-offs are made among business units, and they're not always simple choices. You have to understand all of the factors that contribute to the relative value of each unit under consideration. If the economy is heading downward, for example, which units should take deeper cuts and which ones less? While the answer might seem obvious—spare the unit that earns higher returns—it might be the wrong answer. If the capital market values that particular unit at a lower sustainable price/earnings ratio—say, because it's in a mediocre industry and is earn-ing those returns now only because you were the first to cut costs—you'll want to favor the unit that has more value for the long run.

OUTCOMES OF THE OPERATIONS PROCESS

One outcome of the operations process is identifying targets that clearly and specifically reflect not only what a business wants to achieve but what it is *likely* to achieve—because they are based on the most realistic assumptions and on the hows of achieving them.

Figures 4 and 5 show the outcomes for the business unit we've been discussing. They're clear and specific. They show the sources of change in revenue and operating income over the next twelve months and their relative proportion. (Similarly, in the components-to-selling solution strategic shift discussed in chapter 6, the account manager and the engineering people were dependent upon each other to shape the value proposition.)

In addition to clear targets, the operations process yields a lot of learning. The leaders who participate in the reviews are thinking about and debating the very guts of the business. They get to see the company as a whole and how each of their moving parts fits into it. They learn how to allocate and reassign resources when the environment changes.

Operating reviews are superb coaching sessions. Operations may have five hundred lines in the budget: Which ones are more significant? What are their relationships? There is no formula for answering these questions, and there never will be one. In the process of working these things out with the leader, people get practice in making the trade-offs, balancing the short and long term.

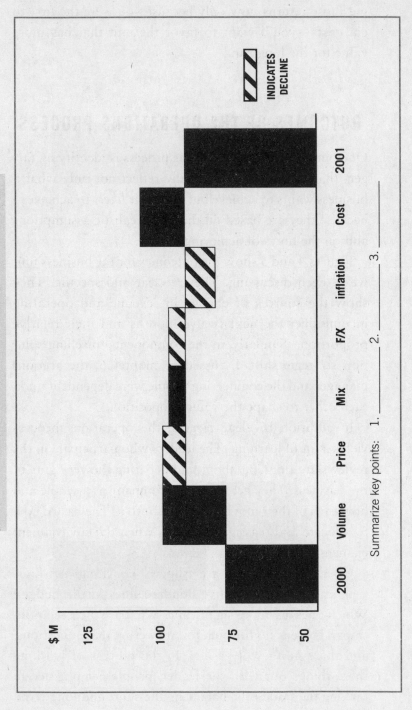

FIGURE 4: OPERATING INCOME BRIDGE

INDICATES DECLINE

$ M
125
100
75
50

2000   Volume   Price   Mix   F/X   Inflation   Cost   2001

Summarize key points: 1. _____   2. _____   3. _____

252

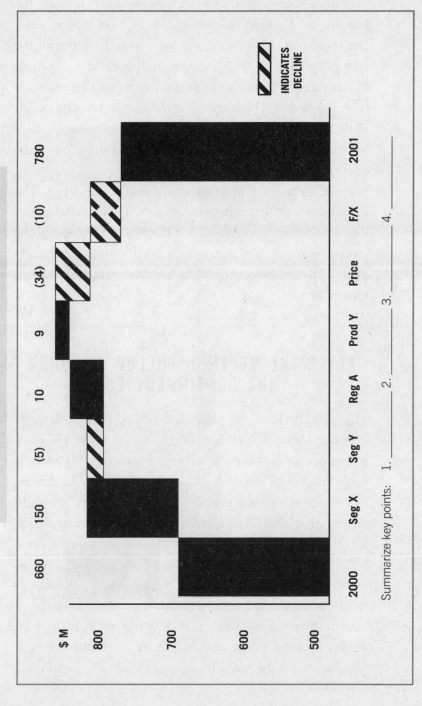

FIGURE 5: REVENUE BRIDGE 2001

	660	150	(5)	10	9	(34)	(10)	780
$ M								
800								
700								
600								
500								
	2000	Seg X	Seg Y	Reg A	Prod Y	Price	F/X	2001

INDICATES DECLINE

Summarize key points: 1. _____ 2. _____ 3. _____ 4. _____

253

In this social environment, people also acquire the knowhow of asking incisive questions, and leaders exercise their skills in encouraging inquiry and getting all the viewpoints out. Threading the dialogues into a whole builds relationships among leaders running various parts of the company. The leaders can then bring the same skills to their own reviews, energizing their people and expanding their capacities. This builds the social software of the organization.

Finally, the operations process builds confidence. The team knows they can meet the targets. They have the flexibility to adapt to changes, and they've gone through the moves required to succeed in all but the most drastically altered circumstances. In effect, they've trained in a flight simulator.

AFTER THE MEETING: FOLLOW-THROUGH AND CONTINGENCIES

Any good review ends with closure and follow-through. Without them, you're apt to get one of those meetings where people nod their heads in agreement, only to start wriggling out of the deals a few days later. The leader has to be sure that each person has carried away the right information and taken accountability for what he or she agreed to do.

One powerful technique is to send each person a memo outlining the details of the agreements. Here are excerpts from one such letter, sent by Larry to an AlliedSignal component after the review of the 1999 operating plan. Sales for the business in question had been good and were getting better, so the main focus was on driving for higher margins.

November 25, 1999
To: Leaders of Group X
From: Larry Bossidy

Thank you for a solid review of your 1998 AOP [annual operating plan]. Here are some observations that you should share with your business leaders.

- For 1999, build a plan that allows you to react to different scenarios, given the high level of economic uncertainty.
- Given this uncertainty, we need an ambitious plan for productivity that overachieves the target.
- Develop a proposal for reducing your cost structure. I want to know what you would do, how much it would cost, and the impact to census and 1999 AOP financials.
- Our quality problems are disturbing. Continue to work to improve quality. I am especially concerned with our problems with customer X. Develop a program for X that will convince them that we are addressing the issues. A key component of the solution is a further reduction in our supply base.
- Good work on reducing past-due shipments. However, past-dues are still among the highest in the company, so opportunity remains.
- Supply chain is our number-one process priority. Do not fix the problems individually; fix the process. Please make sure we have a defined path to achieve the reduction in the fourth quarter.
- The $36 million price reduction is an area that needs continuous review to find creative ways to reduce the impact.
- Cost reduction is a big opportunity for you. One point of cost will take you from an uncomfortable position to a comfortable one.

BUSINESS A

- You need to do something about quality. Thirty percent customer returns is way too high. Devote more resources in engineering to get at the quality issues.
- It does not appear that we are realizing the upside associated with price increases in the aftermarket. Let's understand why we are not seeing it and, if there are cost issues, develop plans to mitigate it.
- Make sure we have a plan to improve repair and overhaul margins, particularly on commercial propulsion products.
- We need to drive better results out of product line Z.
- Given that the risks you identified are likely, we need a well-thought-out contingency plan that focuses on costs.

MANUFACTURING OPERATIONS

- Under normal economic conditions, your material plans would be fine, but in this disinflationary environment we need more. Work with executive A to crisp up your plans. You have a lot of opportunity here. I would like your targets to be more aggressive.
- Your inventory target is not aggressive enough. Work with executives A and B to determine your inventory entitlement and develop a more credible plan with aggressive targets. Keep in mind that you can't reduce inventories without reducing lead times. A significant reduction is needed in Q4 to achieve the cash flow target.
- I would like you to put more focus on Six Sigma projects. Let's be sure we are realizing the value of the black-belt/green-belt resources.
- We have had success driving productivity at product line B, but it has been at the expense of working cap-

ital. Figure out how we can drive productivity using less working capital.

1999 AOP TARGETS

Here are your revised targets (based on assumptions that are consistent with your plan submission):

Overall you had a great AOP presentation last week. It was obvious that manufacturing component A has a good understanding of its businesses. I would like to thank you and your team for all the hard work. Let's get back together on December 9 to discuss the specifics of how we will achieve the targets as well as the alternatives for our D, E, and F businesses.

■ ■ ■

Two other parts of follow-through are contingency plans and quarterly reviews.

Contingency Plans

Companies that execute can put a contingency plan into effect on the turn of a dime—recall how Honeywell responded to the crisis of September 11. When the Asian contagion roiled world economies in 1997, both AlliedSignal and GE created contingency plans and redid their budgets in six weeks. They had this capability because they had thought about it beforehand and had been practicing the process for years.

LARRY: The operating plan is done. Now the leadership looks at the assumptions that might be most vulnerable and plans for contingencies in case results start to come up short. For example, we'll calculate that if a business misses its growth target of 10 percent, it will cost us revenues of X and margins of Y. So we'll have an idea of the magnitude of costs we would have to take out and the productivity gains we'd have to increase to make up for the shortfall. We don't get very granular, but our people are very adaptable. They know the kinds of actions they'll have to take to adjust, when and if.

Quarterly Reviews

Quarterly reviews help keep plans up to date and reinforce synchronization. They also give a leader a good idea about which people are on top of their businesses, which ones aren't, and what the latter need to do.

LARRY: I'll go with my HR person to a business, especially one I don't know well, and before starting on the business plan, we'll meet with the general manager and his HR person to go over the people- and organization-development plans. I'll also try to make the point that the strategy is appropriate and is being translated into the business plan. Then we'll go through the operating plans in terms of most recent quarter: sales, market growth, exogenous factors, margins, levels of expense. I like to do it with a lot of people where I can get dialogue from a large constituency. The better the people, I find, the more they like these reviews. Later I hold a public forum, assembling a group of people in an auditorium, on a loading dock, or whatever, to talk about what the company is trying to do and take questions. On the plane home, I write a note about what we agreed to in the quarterly review.

The review itself is a basis to compare how the general manager has done against the first quarter plan. I might learn that we need to adjust the plan. Maybe he says to me, "I missed my sales in the first quarter because it's a slow season." I'd say, "Well, wait a minute, it was a slow season last year in the first quarter too. So what does that have to do with anything?" And perhaps he'll say, "But I know I'm going to pick up my sales in the second quarter. I'll be on plan by the end of the second or third quarter." I then have to ask, "Let's assume you're not. That means I don't do anything about it until the fourth quarter after you don't make it in the third quarter. Well, let's not do that. Let's start doing something now as though you're not going to make the sales budget. If you do, all the better and you're ahead of your plan and that's great, but if you don't you're protected." Same thing with productivity. If someone says, "I didn't have a good first quarter, but I will have in the second," again I have to say, "Well, let's assume you don't. What are you going to do now about that?"

My purpose is to set up with him or her an apparatus to still achieve that plan by the end of the year. I explore the first quarter in detail to see how much they know about it and what they're going to do about it. And the emphasis that I have is on early action.

What I say is, "People, we're talking about operating plans. This is not about hopes and dreams. This is about realities. Don't tell me you hope it's going to get better. Don't tell me that you dream about doing it better. The reality is that in the first quarter it wasn't better. That's the database that we're going to go from, and that's the database we're going to act upon."

Now, if it develops that we can foresee some cash issues at the end of the second quarter, I might reduce the capital budget a little bit. I'm going to say, "Okay, we approved

$50 million for capital expenditures in your operating plan, but I'm going to reduce that to $45 million in order to maintain our cash flow plan. Now you have to select the capital projects most beneficial to the business. If you're back on plan at the end of the quarter, fine, we'll look at those things again, and we may bring them back to the original state."

This process doesn't guarantee that you make every plan in the corporation—you don't. But you'd be surprised by the number of people who come awfully close under conditions that were a lot different than were assumed when they put the plan together.

GOALS TO LIVE BY

As we noted earlier, a big problem with conventional budget processes is that targets disconnected from reality can be all but meaningless for the people who have to meet them. An operations process that runs on the social software of execution solves this problem, because the people themselves help set realistic targets. And since those targets are the ones their rewards are linked to, the operating plan is where they take full ownership of them. This is the bedrock of accountability.

LARRY: Let's assume we rolled up the operating plan, and the corporation was $50 million short of what it had to do in order to meet the estimates of the street and so on. I tell them, "We as a company think this is the realistic target. This is what we've led people to believe. We've asked you to come up from what we agreed upon earlier, but there's still a gap between what you think you can make in the ten operating businesses and what we think we have to make."

I can't just give them numbers they can't make, because that isn't going to be helpful. We've got to talk about how we fill the gap. I say, "What ideas do we have that begin to close this gap? We're going to keep health care costs flat across the organization, so that's going to give you two cents a share. I've got some ideas to help you, but I'm still short."

So you have a good debate about how to close whatever gap exists. You want to have that debate because the worst thing is someone who says he can make it but then doesn't. You count on him, and he doesn't come through. I've talked to many operating people who said, "You know, I knew at the beginning we had no chance at this plan." My reply is, "Why didn't you speak up and say so? I'm not going to run out of the room. I *am* going to challenge your plan. I'm going to try to get as much stretch as I can, but if it's not achievable, nothing's been accomplished here that's good."

One approach is to give a person a number, and she comes into a budget review. She says, "You know, I'm highly confident I can make ninety percent of this number in this way. I don't know how I'm going to make the remaining ten percent—I can't see it in the business. But I've got a couple thoughts, and I'll accept your challenge. And I'll come back at the end of the first quarter to tell you whether it's in the cards or not, because if I don't know by then, it's not going to happen."

I'll say to her, "I'll give you a couple of suggestions right now. I've been over your plan. If you get one more point of productivity, that closes the gap. One half-point of price will close the gap. But I don't want you to tell me you're going to get another point of productivity or half-point of price until you go back and make sure you can. And you may have better ways to close the gap. But those are two things to think about."

Last year, for example, one manager organized a specialized sales program to put a product into a new market, adding a couple of people to run it, and it brought us revenue we wouldn't have had otherwise. In another segment we took a risk and were able to increase prices by half a point. And we trained five more Six Sigma black belts, enabling us to have more cost-reduction projects. All these came out of dialogues; I didn't suggest them.

Sometimes, on the other hand, you have to put the pressure on. Say somebody clearly isn't going to make his targets and doesn't have a good excuse. I might say, "So what are we going to do? I've got to report to Wall Street at the end of the quarter, and I can't just walk away from my commitments. Maybe I should bring you along when I go to the press and say, 'Here's the guy who's responsible.' No? Well, how about this: You've got fifteen thousand stock options (I always know how many they have), and you're a member of the 401(k). Your team members also have options and 401(k)s. If we miss our estimate and our stock drops ten or fifteen percent, doesn't that have any impact on you and the others?"

So I make it a personal challenge: if you don't accomplish your objective, if you don't do what you said you were going to do, you are hurting yourself and your teammates. Usually the man will break his chops to make the numbers.

■ ■ ■

This kind of review process lets you set meaningful stretch goals too. Such goals are a popular leadership technique (popular among leaders, anyhow) for getting people to exert maximum effort. But many leaders are far too casual about how they specify and use them.

RAM: There can be a lot of hot air in stretch goals. They are useful, but not if they're arbitrary, if they're used as a tool to whip people into a frenzy of working harder. A stretch goal has basically two purposes. One, it can force you to think about doing things in a radically different way; two, it can help you to execute exceptionally well.

For example, Sam Walton set a stretch goal with his famous declaration: "I will continue to reduce prices as long as I live." He accomplished that. Henry Ford did it in the early 1920s. Matsushita did it in Japan. And Ingvar Kamprad of IKEA did that in Sweden for a long time.

Meeting his stretch goal forced Walton to find new ideas that Sears and Kmart never had: dock-to-dock logistics, online information transfer to suppliers, and cutting out a lot of waste in transactions. These procedures translated into everyday low prices.

The key is to evaluate the plausibility of the stretch goal, and there's a methodology for that. Usually there are fewer than half a dozen factors or assumptions that have to go right, some of them involving luck. Identify those at the time of the debate. Talk about them, and then say, "If all the stars get lined up, we won't miss it. If they don't get lined up, we have a chance to miss it."

LARRY: You want some stretch in your plans. But really you should know how much of a stretch that is. You can't go in and say, "Look, I'm just going to give you a number." My approach is that I want to know how you're going to make your number. First and foremost, I need to see that you have a handle on it. Two, you'll know that I know you have a chance to get it done, so you'll get more resources if you need them. Three, I learn a lot, because the chances are I don't have an answer about the method of accomplishment.

It usually works out nicely. Yes, the numbers are a little higher than people thought possible at first, but they agree to final plans that they think were realistic. Now maybe a person eventually doesn't make her number because the market changes or we did some things that *didn't* work. But if she's worked her business to the optimum, she deserves a bonus. Likewise, I have seen men in good market places not make their number or just make their number when they should have made 10 percent more. I wasn't generous in terms of their bonus allocations.

■ ■ ■

The heart of the working of a business is how the three processes of people, strategy, and operations link together. Leaders need to master the individual processes and the way they work together as a whole. They are the foundation for the discipline of execution, at the center of conceiving and executing a strategy. They are the differentiation between you and your competitors.

The discipline of execution based on the three core processes is the new theory of leadership and organization distilled from practice and abbreviation. We hope you find it useful to change the way you work.

CONCLUSION: LETTER TO A NEW LEADER

Dear Jane,

Congratulations on your promotion! We couldn't be happier for you. We know you are excited about exercising your leadership at a higher level. And we'd like to share with you some information we think will help you with your new challenge.

Start by considering what skills this job requires and how they compare with the ones you have. We're sure you've got the self-confidence to make this kind of candid self-assessment. If you're short on experience in one area (most leaders are at some point in their careers, as you know), be sure you've got someone who's strong in it. Overall, you'll want to put together a team balanced with the different types of talent you need to improve your chances of success.

How well do you know your organization? Make sure you get down where the action is, talking with people at all levels, asking them questions, and listening to the answers. You'll learn much of value about the realities of the business, and you'll establish the personal connection that is a hallmark of a great leader.

Get a good handle early on about the beliefs and behaviors of the people under your direction. Your own behaviors have a great deal to do with your success so far, Jane. You've insisted on boundaryless thinking, you're open to opinions that differ from yours, and you've practiced and led the honest, inclusive dialogues that bring reality into the open. You have also placed a high premium on getting things done, winning, and attracting the very best and most diverse talent.

Are you among like-minded people in your new job? Does this business have an execution culture, one where people get things done because performance is recognized and rewarded? Do people embrace reality and engage in constructive debates? Or is the place full of political gamesmanship, butt-covering, and denial? If so, start creating the social software you'll need to change the culture. It's how you get the whole organization to follow your lead, and it'll be crucial to maintaining your record of high achievement.

Nothing is more important to achieving results than your personal leadership of the three core processes. These are the guts of the business, and they're your levers for changing or reinforcing the culture. The biggest single difference between businesses that execute and those that don't is the rigor and intensity with which the leader prosecutes these processes. You will be pulled in every direction as people want you to meet community leaders, government officials, and suppliers and put you on display in every conceivable venue. But running the processes must be at the top of your priority list.

We know you believe that people are your organization's most important assets, but your stewardship of the people process is what will convert that belief to reality. Make your people process second to none. Your success will be determined by the number of "A" players you have and the extent to which you can harmonize their efforts. You need to know at least the top third of the people in your unit in terms of their performance and their growth potential. You need to be certain that appraisals are honest and direct, and that your people get the feedback, coaching, and training they need to grow. And because compensation is the ultimate driver of performance, you must ensure that your compensation system rewards the doers.

We encourage you to compare your people with those of the competition, to ask whether the performance bar is high enough, and whether people have the necessary discipline to win consistently.

Getting the strategy process right is crucial to your longer-term success and that of your organization. Are business leaders driving the process, or has it been delegated to nerdy and isolated planning types? Does the plan have the right information to allow an accurate assessment of your position versus your competition? Is it sufficiently detailed so that your people can see how they will achieve both growth and productivity improvements? You can't settle for vague declarations in these crucial underpinnings of the plan—you need specific programs. Are the issues confronting the business identified? Does your new team have a track record of overcoming obstacles? As you know, if you don't identify, debate, and resolve the critical issues, the business stalls. Also, are resources allocated in proportion to opportunities, or does every opportunity get some resources and none get enough? Is the plan straightforward, concise, and easily understood? Remember, you want everyone in your business to have a good grasp of it.

You have a budget, but do you have the action plan the budget should represent? We see countless cases where the numbers are assembled painstakingly and presented expertly but have little to do with the reality of running the business. A one-year operating plan sets forth a template for achievement. It synchronizes all of the organization's parts and links them with the strategy and the people processes. It nails down your team's commitments by tying performance explicitly to incentives, so that leaders exercise all the discipline and imagination they can muster to deal with the ever-present unanticipated events.

Jane, we can't stress strongly enough the importance of your personal involvement in these three core processes. You must be in charge from the start of each cycle, to the reviews, and to the follow-up steps you take to make sure the things that are supposed to happen do, in fact, happen. This is how you acquire both the knowledge and the authority to run the business as an integrated, reality-based whole. It is how you ultimately assure that all three processes are linked.

What else do you need to stay on top of? The list can get endless, but three items stand out. First, make sure you and your people really understand your customers: their needs, their buying behaviors, and the changes in those behaviors. Know why they would prefer your products to others. Understanding customers is the base of business success. Second, always look for ways to improve your results by introducing initiatives such as Six Sigma or digitization. They not only can be productive, they can also bind your people together in a common cause. Third, maintain and sharpen your intellectual honesty so that you're always realistic. See things as they are, not the way you want them to be.

It will be hard at times to know how you're doing. We hope your organization gives you the feedback and coaching you will be giving your own reports. But even when that's the case, we have found that a leader needs a confidant, someone outside the business to help her keep her head straight. This person should be someone wise, an individual who will be candid with you and help you to keep asking yourself whether you're growing, learning, and making the tough choices. And take care of yourself. The new job can be stressful, and you need to live a balanced life. Don't let yourself get too low or too high. Consistent behavior is a sign of a contained ego, and inspires confidence in you from those around you.

Above all, Jane, remember that you've earned your leadership by your commitment to the work you've done. Keep that intensity of involvement and deepen it. Some people grow in their jobs, and others swell. The ones who grow are passionate about their businesses. They're never too busy being big honchos to pay attention to the important details and stay close to their people. They're never too high and mighty to listen and learn, to be as curious and inquisitive and open to new ideas as they were the first day of their careers.

This is probably more than you wanted to hear from two old friends. But we take great delight in your progress, and we know you have the talent to do a lot more.

Sincerely,
Larry and Ram

INDEX

Accountability, 22, 23, 48, 88, 92, 106, 176, 177, 260
Adaptability, 198
Airline industry, 241–42
Alcatel (co.), 45
Allaire, Paul, 41
AlliedSignal, 27, 130, 189
  appraisals, 134
  contingency plans, 257
  follow-through, 221, 254
  human resources, 167
  ideas at, 216
  problems at, 1–3, 68, 110
  successes at, 111–12
American Standard, 66
Appraisals, 131–36
Armstrong, Michael, 179–80
Asia, 189, 243, 247, 257
Assumptions, 22, 236–44, 251
AT&T, 42, 44, 67, 179–82, 185, 189, 203
A.T. Cross, 192
A.T. Kearney, 47, 51
Authenticity, 81
Auto industry, 235–36, 243

Batch production manufacturing, 16–17
Baxter International, 168–72
Beliefs, 89–91

Bell Labs, 42, 43, 54
Bombardier (co.), 193
Bonuses, 95–96
Brown, Dick, 46–54, 63, 89, 92–93, 105, 127
Budgets, 228–33, 260, 261, 268
Building to order, 17
Burnham, Dan, 111
Business environment, 4, 5, 15, 30
Business Process Management, 51
Business skills, 173

Cable & Wireless, 46
Candor, 103, 106
Capellas, Michael, 16
Cell phones, 110
CEOs (chief executive officers), 14–15
  See also specific people
Change, 8, 15, 19
Character, 78
Cisco Systems, 42, 239–40
Coaching, 74–78, 86, 229, 251
Colgate-Palmolive, 15, 154, 201, 235, 250
Collaboration, 93–94
Collins, Art, 121
Comcast, 180

Communication, 29, 98
Compaq, 15–16, 17, 18, 20, 21, 110
Compensation, 50, 73, 92–96, 267
Competition, 5, 187–88, 193–95, 210–12, 240, 267
Computer services outsourcing, 46
Conference calls, 48–49, 106
Contingency plans, 257–58
Continuous Improvement Summary, 152–54
Corporate culture, 85–108
Corporate-level strategy, 183–84
Critical issues, 201–4, 236
Customers, 190–91, 239, 268

Decision-making, 97, 123–25
Dell, Michael, 16, 110
Dell Computer, 16, 17, 18, 110, 203–4, 235
Dialogue:
  and art of trade-offs, 249–50
  as basic, 25
  honest, 63, 172–77
  robust, 23, 102–5, 106, 232, 233
Differentiation, 95
Digital Equipment Company (DEC), 15
Dignity, 165–66
Distribution, 240
Duke Energy, 172–77
Dunlap, "Chainsaw Al," 29, 96

Earnings per share, 246, 250
Economy, 240, 242, 250
EDS (co.), 46–54, 63, 89–91, 92–94
Education, 77–78
Einstein, Albert, 32
EMC (co.), 204
Emerson Electric, 5, 15, 112, 201, 250
Emotional fortitude, 78–83, 123
E Solutions, 51
Europe, 144, 243

Execution:
  building blocks of, 55–137
  and change, 8, 19
  and competition, 5
  culture, 4, 30–31
  definition of, 20
  difference made by, 35–54
  discipline of, 3, 6, 7, 21–23, 34
  instinct for, 35
  and leadership, 24–29, 57–84
  milestones for, 197–98
  need for, 11–54
  neglect of, 31
  and results, 20
  social software of, 96–102, 105–6
  and strategy, 195–97
  world class, 5
Executive Jets, 193
Experience, 83–84

Failures, 15, 19
Feedback, 74, 93
Finances, 204–5, 228–33, 260, 261, 268
Follow-through, 71–73, 106, 127–28, 221–24, 254–60
Ford, Henry, 263
Fractionals, 241
Functional skills, 173

Gateway (co.), 16
GE. See General Electric
GE Medical, 191–92
General Electric (GE), 1, 2, 3, 19
  contingency plans, 257
  follow-through, 127
  Jones's naming of Welch, 117–18
  leadership development, 112, 121
  people process, 107, 155–56, 184
  productivity, 250
  realism in management, 22
  Social Operating System, 99–101
  strategy process, 183–84, 189
  strategy review, 207–8

as superior in execution, 5, 15
synchronization, 235
"vitality curve," 93
General Motors (GM), 211–12, 213, 235–36
GE Power Systems, 122–23
Gerstner, Louis V., 20, 39, 121
Goals, 37, 38, 69–71, 94–95, 234, 236–44, 260–64
Gross margins, 246–47
Growth, 191–93, 213–14

Harmony, 103
Hewlett-Packard, 18
Home Depot, 122
Honeywell International:
    assessments, 135, 157–59, 166
    contingency plans, 257
    critical issues, 201–2, 204
    follow-through, 221
    getting back on track, 1, 3–4
    learning strategy, 77
    linking rewards to performance, 94, 95
    operations process, 240–44, 247–49, 257
    people process, 60, 64, 154
    productivity, 250
    Social Operating System, 101
    strategy process, 186, 187, 188, 197, 220
Human resources. See People process; Personnel
Humility, 82–83

IBM, 20, 39, 46
Ideas, 214–17
IKEA (co.), 263
Immelt, Jeff, 19, 112, 121
Indecisiveness, 97
Indonesia, 142–43
Inertia, 155
Informality, 103
Information technology services, 46–47
Innovator's dilemma, 44
Integrity, 25
Intel (co.), 200

Intellectual challenge, 31–32
Interviews, 128–29
Inventory turns, 17–18, 65–66
Involvement, 28, 29, 57–66, 107, 227–28, 268
Iridium consortium, 203

Jack: Straight from the Gut (Welch), 83
Johnson, Larry, 155
Johnson & Johnson, 5
Jones, Reginald, 117–18
Judgment, 26
Juniper Networks, 43

Kampouris, Emmanuel, 66
Kamprad, Ingvar, 263
Kelleher, Herb, 28–29
Kraemer, Harry M. Jansen, Jr., 168, 169

Leaders and leadership:
    behavior of, 105–8, 146–47
    broadening people through coaching, 74–78
    creating framework for cultural change, 85–108
    decisiveness, 123–25
    emotional fortitude, 78–83
    energizing of people, 121–23
    execution as job of, 24–29
    follow-through, 71–73, 127–28
    getting things done through others, 125–27
    importance of involvement, 28, 29, 57–66, 107, 227–28, 268
    letter to new leader, 265–69
    putting right people in right job, 109–37
    setting goals and priorities, 69–71
    six essential behaviors, 57–84
    skills, 173
    See also specific companies and leaders
Leadership Assessment Summary, 150–51, 152

Learning, 251
Lucent Technologies, 20,
    41–45, 54, 69–70, 132
Lutz, Bob, 211–12, 235–36

Management resource reviews
    (MRRs), 157, 158
Management skills, 173
Market segment mapping,
    192–93
Market share, 187
Matsushita (co.), 263
McGinn, Richard, 20, 41–43,
    45
McNerny, Jim, 121
Media One, 181
Micromanagement, 27
Microsoft, 195
Milestones, 197–98
Motorola, 110, 203

Nardelli, Bob, 122–23
National Association of
    Corporate Directors, 20
Nobel Prize winners, 32
Nokia (co.), 110
Norris, Paul, 111
Nortel (co.), 42, 44

Ollila, Jorma, 110
Operationalizing culture,
    89–91
Operations process, 22, 23, 25,
    268
  art of trade-offs, 249–51
  building budget in three days,
    231–33
  building plan, 244–49
  contingency plans, 257–58
  follow-through, 254–60
  goals to live by, 260–64
  importance of synchroniza-
    tion, 234–36
  link with people and strategy
    processes, 148–49, 217–22,
    226–51
  outcomes, 251–54
  quarterly reviews, 258–60
  sound assumptions and realis-
    tic goals, 236–44
Optical gear, 43

Palmisano, Samuel, 20
PCs (personal computers), 16,
    17–18, 203–4
People process, 22, 23, 25,
    26–27, 107–8, 267
  and behavior of leaders,
    146–47
  candid dialogue, 172–77
  Continuous Improvement
    Summary, 152–54
  dealing with nonperformers,
    163–66
  failures, 141–43
  Leadership Assessment
    Summary, 150–51, 152
  linking human resources to
    business results, 166–72
  link with strategy and opera-
    tions processes, 148–49,
    212, 217–22
  matching right person with
    right job, 144–45
  retention risk, 154–55
  succession depth, 154, 155
  See also Personnel
Perot, Ross, 47
Personal connection, 64–65
Personnel, 50–51, 80–81
  doers as preferred employees,
    119–21
  honest appraisals, 131–36
  lack of knowledge about,
    113–14
  lack of right people in right
    job, 113–18
  leaders' lack of personal com-
    mitment, 118
  meeting commitments,
    131–34
  nonperformers, 115–16,
    163–66
  psychological comfort factor,
    116–18
  putting right people in right
    job, 109–37
  quality of, 109–10
  See also People process
Pfeiffer, Eckhard, 15–16, 20
Pfizer (co.), 200–201
PLM Solutions, 51
Poses, Frederic M., 111

Principle of simultaneity, 232
Priorities, 69–71, 234
Priory, Rick, 172, 175–76
Procter & Gamble, 213
Productivity, 2, 250

Quality of service, 53
Quarterly reviews, 258–60
Questioning, 74–75

Reality, 22, 67–69, 103–4, 106
Redlinger, Don, 134, 136, 167
Reference-checking, 130–31
Results, 19, 20, 86, 166–72
Retention assessment, 175
Reward. *See* Compensation
Rolfe, Chris, 172–77
Rosen, Ben, 20, 21
Routers, 43

Schacht, Henry, 20, 42
Self-awareness, 81–82
Self-confidence, 82
Self-mastery, 82
Senior slating, 170–71
Simplicity, 70
Six Sigma processes, 30, 60, 61, 77, 95, 197
Social Operating Mechanisms, 98–101, 208
Social Operating System, 99
Southwest Airlines, 15
Stock options, 95
Strategy, 7, 15, 21
Strategy process, 22, 23, 25, 267
    assessment of external environment, 189–90
    building blocks, 182–84
    building plan, 184–87
    business execution, 195–97
    business growth, 191–93
    and competition, 193–95
    critical issues, 201–4
    existing customers and markets, 190–91
    and finances, 204–5
    importance of "hows," 179–82

link with people and operations processes, 148–49, 178–206, 212, 217–22
    milestones for executing plan, 197–98
    questions for, 187–206
    short and long term, 198–201
    See also Strategy review
Strategy review, 207–25
    and competition, 210–12
    follow-through, 221–24
    and ideas, 214–17
    and organizational ability to execute strategy, 212–13
    and overreaching, 213–14
    questions to raise at, 209–21
Summe, Gregory L., 111
Sunbeam (co.), 96
Synchronization, 234–36

Tactics, 21–22
Talent reviews, 157–63
Tandem (co.), 15
TCI (co.), 181
Telecommunications Act (1996), 180, 181
Thoman, Richard C., 39–41, 46, 67
Torre, Joe, 83
Trade-offs, 217, 249–51
Trani, John, 191
TRW (co.), 203
Tucker, Mike, 169, 170, 171

Unilever (co.), 214

Values, 89
Velocity, 17, 18, 72
Vitality curve, 93

Wagoner, Rick, 212
Wal-Mart, 15, 235
Walton, Sam, 28–29, 263
Warner-Lambert, 200–201
Welch, Jack, 122, 207
    and dialogue, 101
    and informality, 103
    and inventory turns, 65–66
    Jones's selection of, 117–18

Welch, Jack (*cont.*)
  leadership development, 112, 121
  management style, 22, 28, 29, 107
  mistakes, 83
  strategy process, 183–84
  "vitality curve," 93

Western Electric, 42, 54
Wintel architecture, 15

Xerox, 39–41, 46, 51, 54, 67, 202

Zarella, Ron, 235